On Being Human

Other Books by
ERICH FROMM
from Continuum

Marx's Concept of Man

The Art of Being

The Art of Listening

The Essential Fromm

To Have Or to Be?

· ERICH FROMM ·

On Being Human

Foreword by
RAINER FUNK

continuum
NEW YORK · LONDON

2005

The Continuum International Publishing Group Inc
15 East 26th Street, New York, NY 10010

The Continuum International Publishing Group Ltd
The Tower Building, 11 York Road, London SE1 7NX

Printed in the United States of America

Library of Congress Cataloging-in-Publication Data

Fromm, Erich, 1900–1980
    On being human / Erich Fromm ; foreword by Rainer Funk
    p.   cm.
    Selections from Fromm's unpublished writings.
    Includes bibliographical references and index.
    ISBN 0-8264-1005-7 (pbk : alk. paper)
    1. Humanistic psychology. 2. Humanism—20th century.
    3. Social psychology. 4. Psychoanalysis. I. Title,
BF204.F756   1994
150.19'57—dc20   93-9243
    CIP

Contents

Editor's Foreword

Whoever attempts to identify the "scarlet thread" that runs through the entire corpus of Fromm's writings will, first of all, discover the sociopsychological approach by which he searched for man's socially molded passionate strivings. Yet, no later than the late 1930s, in conjunction with his departure from the Institute for Social Research and his disputes with Horkheimer, Marcuse, and Adorno, something different and unmistakably Frommian becomes noticeable and runs through his life and work like a scarlet thread: his *humanistic* view of man and the world. Whenever Fromm wants, from this point on, to characterize even his own thought, he uses the attribute "humanistic." He speaks of a humanistic science of man, of humanistic socialism, of humanistic industrial society, of humanistic conscientiousness, of humanistic religion, of humanistic management, of a humanistic view of the world, of humanistic psychoanalysis, of humanistic character, of humanistic ethics, and of humanistic utopia.

In evaluating Fromm's thought, it is often exactly this humanistic belief in man that leads to a "parting of the minds": How can Fromm, who has recognized the deleterious effects of man's self-alienation with such clarity, and who has explained them in terms of our culture's socio-economic relationships—and yet has simultaneously unmasked any salvation *from without* as merely an expression of self-alienation—how can Fromm nevertheless believe in man?

The texts of this volume from Fromm's unpublished writings answer this question in a twofold manner: They show the entire extent of the destructive and terrible self-alienation of today's man, and yet simultaneously they speak of the real possibilities that can lead to man's becoming happy. There is a "real" utopia as long as man has at least partial access to his own powers that promote growth.

The departure point of Fromm's humanism, made possible by the insights of psychoanalysis, is that the unconscious represents the entire person—and all of humanity. The unconscious contains the entire spectrum of possible answers, and it very much matters which possibilities are cultivated and which are hindered and repressed. Fundamentally, though, ". . . man, in any culture, is faced by a gamut of possibilities: He is the archaic man, the beast of prey, the cannibal, the idolater; but he is also the being with the capacity for reason, for love, for justice."[1] Since man does not exist except as a social being, the particular type of society in which he lives determines which possibilities are favored. Every society shapes the energies of people in such a way that they *want* to do what they *must* do in order for society to function. "Social necessities become transformed into personal needs, into the 'social character.'"[2]

Yet every society does not only promote certain possibilities that are at the disposal of humans' unconscious, insofar as society makes these possibilities known and the individual identifies with them. Possibilities and tendencies that contradict social patterns of behavior—the character of society—are quelled and repressed. That is why "our conscious mind represents mainly our own society and culture, while our unconscious represents the universal man in each of us."[3]

In his unconscious, man experiences all humanity and himself as "saint and sinner, child and adult, sane and insane, man as

---

1. E. Fromm, "Humanism and Psychoanalysis," in *Contemporary Psychoanalysis*, Vol. 1 (1964), p. 27.
2. Ibid., pp. 75–76.
3. E. Fromm, *The Heart of Man: Its Genius for Good and Evil, in Religious Perspectives* (Vol. 12), ed. Ruth Nanda Anshen, New York, 1964, p. 93.

he was in the past and man as he will be in the future."[4] This condition is why humanism has its ultimate justification in humanistic experience, that is, in the humanizing and productive effect of making conscious that which is unconscious. Writes Fromm:

> This humanistic experience consists in the feeling that nothing human is alien to one, that "I am you," that one can understand another human being because both of us share as our common possession the same elements of human existence. . . . The broadening of self-awareness that humanistic experience brings about—including as it does the transcending of consciousness and the revelation of the sphere of the social unconscious—enables man to experience himself in the full dimensions of his shared humanity.[5]

Thus, with the knowledge that the unconscious, independent of that which is socially conscious and repressed, represents the entire person with all his possibilities, Fromm justifies the humanistic belief in the unity of people not only theoretically; as soon as one opens oneself to one's unconscious, becomes conscious of one's unconscious and thus comes to experience one's other possibilities, one then unfurls, grows, and has the paradoxical and productive—or, as Fromm also says, the humanistic—experience that one can be related reasonably and lovingly to the world and to people because nothing foreign is any longer really strange to one. Only in opening oneself up to the unconscious, to the entire person in oneself, in the realization of one's individuality, does a person come to the experience of the universal human, for "only the fully developed individual self can abandon the ego."[6]

What interests Fromm most about humanism, what leads him to use the attribute "humanistic" so often, and why he

---

4. Ibid.
5. Ibid.
6. E. Fromm, *Beyond the Chains of Illusion: My Encounter with Marx and Freud,* in *Credo Perspectives,* ed. Ruth Nanda Ashen, New York, 1962, p. 178. ·

advocates a renaissance of humanism has to do with this humanistic experience. He is concerned with what is humanistic in the sense of the development of man's own loving and reasonable powers, as well as with a humanistic orientation and attitude (as he made clear within his characterology) by his concept of productivity and of productive orientation, of biophilia and the mode of being. As a person experiences himself more and more as author, actor, and subject of his life—and is thus *himself* who thinks, feels, and acts with his *own* forces—he also develops his forces of reason and love, with which he can be entirely with the world and other persons without losing himself.

The individual texts of this volume were composed during the last twenty years of Fromm's life. These texts were characterized as much by the insight into the entire extent of humans' self-alienation as by a faith, unbroken to the very end, in man. They are based on lectures (especially Part I) and manuscripts that Fromm formulated for specific occasions (especially Part II, which contains humanistic initiatives and declarations) or that he wrote as book manuscripts (such as the concluding Part III, concerning the real utopia of the being mode of existence, according to Meister Eckhart and Karl Marx).

The editor has provided the grouping, coordination, and division of the texts, as well as most of their titles. Editorial notes concerning the origin of the individual manuscripts appear in cursive script and precede the texts. As in all unpublished writings, several omissions and additions are made easily recognizable by brackets.

Tübingen, 1993   Rainer Funk

(Translated by Lance W. Garmer)

· PART I ·

The Humanistic Alternative

· 1 ·

Modern Man and the Future

From September 6 through 11, 1961, an International Congress for Psychoanalysis and Its Continued Development took place in Düsseldorf, West Germany. Aside from Fromm, participants included a group of "non-orthodox" psychoanalysts from Germany (W. Schwidder, F. Heigl, and F. Riemann of the German Psychoanalytical Society, to name only three), the Netherlands (A. J. Westerman-Holstijn), Switzerland (H. Binswanger and M. Boss of Dasein-Analysis), and the United States (G. Chrzanowski and H. Stierlin). On September 6, before these some 300 non-orthodox psychoanalysts, Fromm presented a lecture (published in his German Gesamtausgabe, *1966b) on the "Fundamental Positions of Psychoanalysis." A second, public lecture by Fromm took place on September 9. Its title was "Modern Man and His Future." This lecture contained a condensed version of Fromm's diagnosis of the age at the beginning of the 1960s, before he had developed the concept of "necrophilia." The present text, published here for the first time in English, is a transcription of a tape of that lecture. Fromm delivered the lecture largely without the use of a manuscript.*

To talk today [in 1961] on the topic "Modern Man and His Future" means not only that one must ask what the future of

15

man will be, but also whether man will have any future whatsoever. At the same time, this question about the future pertains not only to modern man and his civilization; in view of the growing destructive force of atomic weapons, the issue concerns man's life on this Earth in general. Certainly this is the first time in the history of man that one must pose such a question. The atomic bomb is modern society's worst symptom of disease.

What do I mean by "modern man"? By this, one can mean either man of today—that is, *all men* of the twentieth century—or man in the Western industrialized countries as opposed to man in Asia, Africa, and the non-industrialized parts of the world. In asking what I mean by "modern man," it becomes clear that something in the historical situation has also changed for the first time: People of the non-industrialized countries are more and more quickly coming to resemble the people of the West. Western man has exported his technology and certain ideas to the as-yet-non-industrialized countries. Yet because the West seems to be losing, or has already lost, the power over the world that it had for centuries, it is engaged in transforming the entire world according to its own Western development.

When I speak of the West's own development, then I primarily mean Western technology and industry, as well as the Western idea of historical progress and of a historical goal. Nationalism, a relatively recent Western product, is also a part of the development of the West. These ideas have established themselves in the East often in the form of a perverted Marxism or Socialism.

What is happening today is perhaps something similar to when Christianity was grafted from Rome onto a pagan Europe. Rome did, indeed, lose its political power, yet it had imbedded its culture, its ideas, and its forms of organization in foreign soils. These soils were at that time much more primitive than today's pre-industrial peoples are in comparison to the West.

Stages in the Development of Western Man

To give a complete overview of the most important stages of Western development within the confines of a lecture can be accomplished here only by suggestion and schematically, yet the overview is a prerequisite for understanding what will follow.

(1) The first stage in the development of Western man spans the time from approximately 1500 B.C. until the beginning of the Christian age. This stage is characterized by man's great turn from idolatry to humanistic religion. I will come back to what I mean by "idolatry"; I only want to say here that by idolatry I mean that form of man's search for unity in which he returns to nature, to his own "animalness," submitting himself. He submits himself to nature, to the work of his own hands (in the form of idols made of gold and silver or of wood) *or* he submits himself to other people.

The turn from idolatry to humanistic religion presumably begins with the religious revolution of Akhnaten [or Amenophis IV, Egyptian emperor, 1375–1358 B.C.] and then continues in Mosaic religion, in Taoism, in Buddhism, and in the Classical period of Greek philosophy. All these developments are directed toward a *salvation* of man, by means of which man seeks a new unity not, as in the primitive religions of totemism or of animism, through gods of nature and idols made by his own hands, but through pressing forward and finding a new unity with the world by man's complete development. The first stage in the development of Western man is made with the turn toward humanistic religion during these fifteen centuries that, seen historically, are nothing more—to use the words of the writers of the Psalms—than a "watch in the night."

(2) The second stage is reflected in the notion of a *historical* redemption, such as one finds in the message of prophetic messianism. Very simply stated, prophetic messianism developed the following idea: Man was at one with nature in Paradise, but he was—like the animals—without consciousness of his self.

In the act of disobedience against God's commandment, or—we may say—in the ability to say "No," man becomes aware of his self and takes the first steps into freedom. With this step, human history is made for the first time. Man's original harmony with nature is broken. Man is driven from Paradise and is hindered from returning by two angels with flaming swords.

According to this prophetic-messianic notion, history is, in a sweeping sense, a history of reconciliation; it is the history of man's development toward his humanity, toward the development of his specifically human qualities of reason and of love. Once man has completely and fully developed himself, he finds a new harmony, a harmony of the developed, reasonable, self-aware, loving individual who becomes one with the world and yet is an individual. The new harmony is the old harmony, yet on a different level. It is a harmony—yet one entirely different from the harmony man had before his departure from Paradise.

(3) In Christianity, this new prophetic-messianic notion of history as "reconciliation" is transferred from the soil of Palestine to Europe. In the process, its form—the form of the prophetic-messianic notion—is changed somewhat. The most important change is that man's salvation, the changing of humanity, does not take place within history but, rather, transcends it. The Kingdom of God is understood not in a messianic sense, as it is by most of the biblical prophets—namely, as a change of *this* world—but rather as the establishment of a new, spiritual world that transcends this world!

In spite of this modification, the Christian doctrine of reconciliation is a continuation of the thought of prophetic messianism and is, in this sense, distinct from other doctrines of reconciliation, such as Buddhism, since, according to the Christian doctrine, reconciliation is always a collective reconciliation, a salvation of humanity and not merely of the individual. Even if the Christian doctrine of salvation alters a crucial point of the messianic idea of salvation, insofar as a salvation *beyond* history replaces a historical one, it must nevertheless be emphasized that the history of Christianity has repeatedly given impetus to the historical liberation of man—particularly within pre- and post-Reformation Christian sects.

(4) The message of the Gospel, the Good News, is led historically into the current of the Catholic Church. Here, in the Catholic Church, a union of great historical significance was achieved: The Jewish notion of reconciliation, in the form of prophetic messianism, was coupled with the Greek idea of science, of theory. This union of the prophetic-messianic notion of reconciliation with Greek thought—let us say, the philosophies of Aristotle and Plato—constituted something new, something that grew to fruition in Europe over the course of 1,000 years. This process of fruition lasted from the end of pagan Rome [in the 4th century] until the end of the European Middle Ages. For approximately 1,000 years, Europe was pregnant with a Greco-Roman and Judeo-Christian legacy. Then, after 1,000 years, something new was born from the loins of Europe: modern society.

(5) Modern society begins with the Renaissance. According to Carl Jacob Burckhardt's famous formulation, the Renaissance is characterized by the discovery of the individual and of nature. Perhaps instead of saying "discovery," one should more precisely say "re-discovery," since it is the rebirth of much that Greek and Roman antiquity felt about man and nature. The Renaissance was also the birth of a new science.

The Renaissance continued to maintain the messianic-prophetic vision in a new form: in the form of utopia. If prophetic messianism saw the perfect society—the good, humane society—standing at the end of time, the Renaissance utopia sees the good society standing at the end of *space,* somewhere in an as-yet-undiscovered part of the earth. One needs to mention here the utopias of Thomas More, who created the word "utopia" for this kind of vision, of Tommasso Campanella, and of the German Johann Valentin Andreä. From the Renaissance until the end of the nineteenth century, Western thought can be characterized by, among many other things, the fact that utopia as a special version of the messianic vision occupies a central place. In fact, the same can also be said of the ideas of Karl Marx, except that Marx always resisted any suggestion of utopia and never gave it the positive expression that the great utopic writers accorded it. . . .

The man of the Renaissance becomes aware of his power and begins to free himself from the shackles of nature and to dominate it. In the course of subsequent centuries, the new science and the new attitude toward life lead to a true discovery of the world, to a new technology and industry, and to the world's domination by man. In the seventeenth and eighteenth centuries, the new humanism reaches its apogee. Western thought is centered on man, on humanity, and on humaneness. In religious attitudes, theistic concepts recede, yet religious experience as reality is stronger than at any other time except the thirteenth century. The American historian Carl L. Becker has rightly emphasized that the eighteenth century was not less religious than the thirteenth, even if the eighteenth expressed the same religious experience in a different language and in different concepts.

The nineteenth century seemed to draw near to an age of fulfillment: Man had grown to fruition from the end of the Middle Ages to the nineteenth century. The age of fulfillment was supposed to produce the man who dominated nature, would eradicate war, and would produce—as a means to humanity's development—material affluence. The messianic vision of the good society, of the human society, appeared to come to fruition in the nineteenth century. Until the First World War, European humanity was ruled by its belief in the fulfillment of these hopes and ideas. These same hopes and ideas had lost neither their power nor their influence even from the time of the prophets.

What has happened since then? What happened to Western man in the last 60-odd years? There were two world wars, there was the inhumanity of Hitler's system and of Stalinism, and there is the immediate danger of man's total obliteration. If, for centuries, man had hope for the future, he nearly abandoned it after 1914.

I have spoken of the birth process of new societies. I would almost like to say that twentieth-century man seems to be a miscarriage. What has happened, so that everything has seemed to break down at the moment when man appeared to stand at the crowning pinnacle of his historical endeavors?

We know some things about the development that has led to this. What began in the nineteenth century continued in the twentieth with ever-increasing intensity and speed: the growth of the modern industrial system, which led to more and more production and to increased consumer orientation. Man became a collector and a user. More and more, the central experience of his life became *I have* and *I use,* and less and less *I am.* The means—namely, material welfare, production, and the production of goods—thereby became ends. Earlier, man sought nothing but the means for a better life, one that was worthy of human dignity.

The natural bonds of family solidarity and of community dissolved without new ones having been found. Modern man is alone and anxious. He is free, but he is afraid of this freedom. He lives—as the great French sociologist Émile Durkheim has said—in anomie. He is characterized by division or baseness, which makes of him not an individual but an atom, and which no longer individualizes him but atomizes him. "Atom" and "individual" mean the same thing: The first word comes from the Greek, the second from the Latin. The meanings that the words have acquired in our language, however, are opposed. Modern man hoped to become an individual; in reality, he became an anxious atom, tossed to and fro.

The priorities of the industrial system are balance, quantification, and accounting. The question is always: What is worthwhile? What brings profit?

It is necessary to ask such questions in the realm of industrial production. Yet the principles of accounting, of balance, and of profit were, simultaneously, applied to man and have expanded from economics to human life *in toto*. Man has become an enterprise: His life is his capital and his task seems to be to invest this capital as well as possible. If it is well invested, then he is successful. If he invests his life poorly, then he is without success. He himself thus becomes a thing, an object.

We cannot lie to ourselves about this knowledge: When one becomes an object, one is dead, even if one—seen physiologically—is still living. And if one is spiritually dead, although still physiologically alive, then one is not only subject to decay but becomes dangerous—dangerous to oneself and dangerous to others.

People of the nineteenth century were certainly different from those of the twentieth. People of the earlier century were used to either accepting authority or to rebelling against it. Samuel Butler's novel *The Way of All Flesh* (1903) is an excellent illustration of the rebellion of a nineteenth-century man fighting against authority in both the family and in the state. Nineteenth-century man felt it to be a moral duty to collect and to preserve. As is so often the case, this moral idea had its foundation in the methods of production of nineteenth-century society. It was important to accumulate capital.

In the twentieth century, greater and greater criticism arose against certain ideas that had played a large role in the life of the previous century. Today the primary issue is not the competition of people among one another and the antagonisms that result from the spirit of competition. Quite the contrary: People today form a team, a well-oiled group that works smoothly together, since this is the only way that large enterprises can function. Modern industry and economics have effectively developed to the point that, as a requisite for operation, they need people who become consumers, who possess as little individuality as possible, and who are ready to obey an anonymous authority while suffering from the illusion of being free and subject to no authority.

Modern man seeks succour, so to speak, from the Big Mother of the company or of the state and becomes a perpetual infant who, however, can never be satisfied, because he does not develop his possibilities as a person. In the case, particularly, of eighteenth-century France, one already saw that man cannot truly be happy. The words to describe this condition are thus characteristically French: one speaks of a *mal du siècle* and of *malaise*, in order to characterize the distress in a world that is becoming increasingly atomized and more and more senseless. As Émile Durkheim has shown, it is also characteristic that the onset of suicide as a mass phenomenon has to do with this atomization of man and with the process whereby his existence becomes senseless.

Alienation as a Disease of Modern Man

I would now like to discuss somewhat more thoroughly what, in my opinion, is at the crux of this *malaise*, of this *mal du siècle*. The disease from which modern man suffers is *alienation*. The concept of alienation had sunken into oblivion for decades, but it has lately become popular again. Hegel and Marx once used it, and one could rightly say that the philosophy of existentialism is essentially a rebellion against man's growing alienation in modern society.

What, exactly, is alienation? Within our Western tradition, what is meant by alienation has already played a large role—albeit not as the concept "alienation" but rather as the concept "idolatry," in the sense employed by the prophets. Many people naively assume that the difference between so-called idolatry and the monotheistic belief in one true god is merely a numerical matter: The pagans had many gods, while the monotheists believed in only one. This, however, is not the essential difference. According to the prophets of the Old Testament, the essential point is that the idolator is a person who prays to the product of his own hands. He takes a piece of wood. With one part, he builds himself a fire in order, for example, to bake a cake; with the other part of the wood, he carves a figure in order to pray to it. Yet what he prays to are merely things. These "things" have a nose and do not smell, they have ears and do not hear, and they have a mouth and do not speak.

What occurs in idolatry? If one understands idolatry as prophetic thought does, then what occurs is precisely what Freud called *transference*. In my view, transference, as we know it in psychoanalysis, is a manifestation of idolatry: A person transfers his own activities or all of what he experiences—of his power of love, of his power of thought—onto an object outside himself. The object can be a person, or a thing made of wood or of stone. As soon as a person has set up this transferential relatedness, he enters into relation with himself only by submitting to the object onto which he has transferred his own human functions. Thus, to love (in an alienated, idolatrous way) means: I love only when I submit myself to the idol onto which I have transferred all my capacity for love. Or: I am good only when I submit myself to the idol onto which I have transferred my being good. This is the case with wisdom, strength—indeed, with all human characteristics. The more powerful an idol becomes—that is, the more I transfer on it—the poorer I become and the more I am dependent on it, since I am lost if I lose that onto which I have transferred everything that I have.

In psychoanalysis, transference is not essentially different from this. Of course, psychoanalysis is usually concerned with paternal and maternal transferences, because a child sees in its father and mother those persons onto whom it transfers its own experiences. What is essential, however, is not the fact that the child transfers onto his father and mother, but rather the phenomenon of the transference itself—whereby the immature person is searching for an idol. If the person has found an idol to whom or to which he can pray during his entire life, then he need not despair. This is one of the reasons why, in my view, many people so enjoy going to an analyst and never want to leave, *and* why entire societies choose for themselves so-called leaders who are just as hollow and silent as the idols of antiquity, yet who exhort people to transference in order to bind those people to themselves.

Of course, neither Baal nor Astarte exists in modern society. And because we commonly confuse names with things, we are only too happily convinced that things do not exist if their names no longer turn up. In reality, however, we today live in a society that, in comparison to that of earlier centuries, is much more pagan and much more idolatrous.

For Hegel and Marx, "alienation" means that a person has lost himself and has ceased to perceive himself as the center of his activity. A person *has* much and *uses* much, but he *is* little: "The less you *are*, the less you express your life, the more you *have*, the greater is your *alienated* life—and the greater is the saving of your alienated being."[1] A person is not only little, he is nothing, because he is dominated by the things and circumstances that he himself has created. He is the magician's apprentice, Golem. Modern man is controlled by the products of his own hands. He himself becomes a thing. He is nothing, yet he feels big when he feels at one with the state, with production, with the company.

Modern man is constituted by the things that he creates. To illustrate this with an everyday observation: When one sees in person someone whom one knows only from television, one says, "He looks just like he does on television!" Reality is the TV picture; and the correctness of one's perception of how that person really looks is measured against that reality. If he looks

---

1. K. Marx and F. Engels, *Historisch-kritische Gesamtausgabe* [Collected Historico-Critical Works], ed. V. Adoratsky. Part 1, 6 vols. Berlin, 1932, Vol. 3, p. 130. Additional quotes from this edition will be referred to in this volume as MEGA. Cf. E. Fromm, "Economic and Philosophical Manuscripts" in E. Fromm, *Marx's Concept of Man*.

like he does on television, then the perception of reality is true. Reality lies in the thing outside, and the real person is only a shadow of this reality.

Modern man's perception of reality is fundamentally different from that of the people in the [Hans Christian Andersen] fairy tale of "The Emperor's New Clothes." In reality, the emperor is naked, but everyone except the little boy believes he sees the wonderful garments. Everyone is convinced from the beginning that the emperor must have wonderful garments (so he denies his own perception—seeing the emperor naked—and maintains a false image of the emperor). This phenomenon, of seeing the emperor's garments although he is naked, has existed for many millennia. This is how even the stupidest people were able to become regents. They proclaimed their belief that they were wise—and it was, for their people, usually already too late by the time the ruler had to prove his wisdom. In the fairy tale of "The Emperor's New Clothes," the emperor still exists. The issue is only that he is in reality naked, although people believe that he is wearing clothes. Today, though, the emperor is no longer present! Today, man is real only insofar as he is standing somewhere outside. He is constituted only through things, through property, through his social role, through his "persona"; as a living person, however, he is not real.

Atomic weapons are an extremely dramatic and horrible symbol of what alienation is. They are the product of man. They are indeed an expression of his greatest intellectual achievements, yet *they* control *us*. And it has become very questionable whether *we* will ever control *them*. We living people who want to live are becoming powerless, although we are, seemingly, omnipotent humans. We believe that we control, yet we are being controlled—not by a tyrant, but by things, by circumstances. We have become humans without will or aim. We talk of progress and of the future, although in reality no one knows where he is going, and no one says where things are going to, and no one has a goal.

In the nineteenth century, one could say: "God is dead." In the twentieth, one must say that man is dead. Today, this adage rings true: "Man is dead, long live the thing!" Perhaps there is no more ghastly example of this new inhumanity than the presently planned idea for a neutron bomb. What will a neutron weapon do? It will destroy everything that lives and will leave everything that does not live—things, houses, streets— intact. . . .

Indifference as a New Manifestation of Evil

If one considers everything—alienation, man's having become a thing, man's loss of control over himself and his becoming controlled by the things and circumstances that he creates— then one can say that the concept of evil has changed fundamentally. Until now, this was true: Evil is human. All of us are criminals, just as all of us are saints. Each of us is good and each of us is evil. And precisely because evil is also human, we can understand evil, insofar as we see evil in ourselves. This is—or should be—one of the most important abilities of the psychoanalyst: that he not shudder at the evil in others, since he can perceive evil in himself as something human.

Today, something fundamentally different is occurring. Evil no longer exists in contrast to good; rather, there is a new inhumanity: indifference—that is to say, complete alienation, complete indifference vis-à-vis life. I would like to illustrate this new inhumanity with two phenomena: that of Eichmann and that of atomic strategy.

Karl Adolf Eichmann[2] does not give the impression of being particularly evil; rather, he is entirely alienated. He is a bureaucrat for whom it makes no particular difference whether he kills, or whether he takes care of, small children. For him, life has completely stopped being something alive. He "organizes." Or-

_____
2. Nazi leader executed in 1962 in Israel for World War II crimes.

ganization becomes an end in itself, whether it has to do with the gold teeth or the hair of murdered humans or whether it is railroad trains or tons of coal. Anything else is indifferent for him. When Eichmann defends himself and states that he is only a bureaucrat and has, in reality, only regulated trains and worked out schedules, then he is not altogether off the mark. I believe that there is a bit of Eichmann in us all today.

Eichmann's arguments are not all that different from the considerations advanced by today's atomic strategists. I cite as an example Herman Kahn, one of the most important American atomic researchers. Kahn says that it is acceptable if 60 million Americans die during the first three days of an atomic war; if 90 million die, then it is too many. The issue here has to do with the *same* calculating, the *same* balance of life and death as in Eichmann's leading people to their murder.

Mr. Kahn has said something else very horrible that is especially illustrative of what I am speaking about here. Specifically, he has said (before the Subcommittee of the Joint Committee on Atomic Energy on June 26, 1959) and has written in his book *On Thermonuclear War* (1960):

> In other words, war is horrible. There is no question about it. *But so is peace.* And it is proper, with the kind of calculations we are making today, to compare the horror of war *and the horror of peace* and see how much worse it is.[3]

From a clinical point of view, one would characterize as "severely depressed" a person who can say that one must first calculate how much more horrible war is than peace. One would assume that this person is protecting himself from sui-

3. H. Kahn, l.c. p. 47, footnote (italics mine, E. F.). Answering a reporter who questioned this statement, Kahn said, "I meant that the quality of life after a thermonuclear attack would not be much different than before. And who the hell is happy and normal right now? We'd be just about the same after a war—and we'd still be economically useful." (*San Francisco Chronicle,* March 27, 1961.)

cide only by means of such thought. Indeed, one would have to say that this person is insane, and one can pity him. Of course, what *is* horrible is that this person is not an exception, but that millions think as he does. This attitude of the dehumanized human—of the person who does not care, of the person who not only is not his brother's keeper but is not even his *own* keeper—this attitude characterizes modern man.

The Alternative: A Renaissance of Humanism

In view of modern man's disease, is there still any future whatsoever? I believe that there is an answer only in the sense of a choice. I need to preface this with a remark.

If one speaks of *inner lawfulness* in individual and in social life, then there is usually no unilinear causal chain of the type "A causes B." This type of determinism is usually false. One can, however, usually say: A can lead to one, two, three, or four choices, but only to these and no others. We can ascertain and determine that only a certain few choices are possible under the given conditions. Sometimes there are two, sometimes there are more. Without wanting to prophecy anything, I believe that today there is essentially only one choice for modern man and for the people of the earth *in toto:* the choice between barbarism and a new renaissance of humanism.

Because of the present destructive force of atomic weapons, perhaps what some scientists are convinced of is true: that things will never again even come to barbarism, but simply to the extinction of the human race and everything alive. If things do not come to that, then there is the possibility that they will indeed come to barbarism, and to dictatorship, after an atomic war. The survivors will set up a world dictatorship in which all values of the Western tradition will be lost and robots will rule over robots.

The other possibility I see is that the humanism that was about to be born at the end of the nineteenth century will really be born. This assumes that people perceive the inhumanity of their present situation and the danger, not only physical, but most of all spiritual, that is leading them into complete alienation. Their insight would therefore be comparable to one in individual therapy: One must first become aware of who we are, what drives us, and where we are going. Only when we are aware of this can we make a decision about where we *want* to go.

I believe that a humanistic renaissance is possible because all of the prerequisites for it are manifest. The material prerequisites are a given, so that the table can be set for all and no part of the human race must any longer be excluded from it. For the first time, the idea of a unitary humanity has become a reality. It is a fact that, in a historically very short time, man has reached the point at which he must no longer spend the largest part of his powers on nourishing himself as an animal, but can realize the development of his powers as an end in itself. The prerequisites are given, so that the goal may again be the development of mature, creative, loving, and reasonable men. Everything else will be a means subordinate to this goal.

Since I am today still a socialist, as I always was, I believe that the new form of society will be a form of humanistic socialism that is as distinct from existing capitalism as from the falsification of socialism that Soviet communism calls itself. The question, however, is how much more time we have to come to understanding and to change our direction. . . .

One hundred years ago, Ralph Waldo Emerson said: "Things are in the saddle and are riding us." I would like to call attention to the change that Emerson was declaring. For Martin Luther, the question had been whether the devil still sat in the saddle and rode the person. The devil was Evil, and—as I made clear earlier—Evil was still human. For us today, the issue is no longer that the devil is riding us. Our problem is that *things* are riding us—the things, the circumstances that we have created. Adding to Emerson's formulation, one could say: There is a future for modern man only if he puts himself back into the saddle.

(*Translated by Lance W. Garmer*)

· 2 ·

The Psychological Problem of Man in Modern Society

On May 2, 1964, Fromm gave a lecture in Spanish entitled "Problemas psicológicas del hombre en la sociedad moderna" at the Congreso del Centenario, which was organized by the Academia Nacional de Medicina in Mexico City. An English-language version of the Spanish lecture manuscript was among Fromm's unpublished writings; that English-language version was a basis for the present text.

There is a widespread belief in the world that all essential human needs would be fulfilled if the industrial mode of production were perfected, first in the United States and Europe and eventually in Latin America, Asia, and Africa. If man, so goes the assumption, has enough to eat, plenty of leisure time, and an ever-increasing opportunity for consumption, he will be happy and mentally sane.

But more and more voices are being raised today that question this naive optimism. Why is it, so some observers ask, that the most advanced and prosperous countries, such as Sweden and Switzerland, suffer from one of the highest rates of suicide and alcoholism? Why is it that the richest country in the world, the United States, is an example of the fact that we live in the "age of anxiety"?

Why is it that the economically most advanced states in the world threaten each other with total extinction and themselves with total suicide? Is it only because industrialism has not yet achieved all its goals? (The example of Sweden seems to contradict this assumption.) Or is it that there is something fundamentally wrong with industrialism as it has developed both in the capitalist and in the Soviet systems?

Where are we today? The danger of an all-destructive war hangs over humanity, a danger which is by no means overcome by the hesitant attempts of governments to avoid it. But even if man's political representatives have enough sanity left to avoid a war, man's condition is far from the fulfillment of the hopes of the sixteenth, seventeenth, and eighteenth centuries.

Man's character has been molded by the demands of the world he has built with his own hands. In the eighteenth and nineteenth centuries, the character of the middle class showed strong exploitative and hoarding traits. This "active" character was determined by the desire to exploit others and to save one's own earnings to make further profit from them. In the twentieth century, man's character orientation shows considerable passivity and an identification with the values of the marketplace. Contemporary man is certainly passive in most of his leisure time. He is the eternal consumer; he "takes in" drink, food, cigarettes, lectures, sights, books, movies; all are consumed, swallowed. The world is one great object for his appetite: a big bottle, a big apple, a big breast. Man has become the suckler, the eternally expectant and the eternally disappointed.

Insofar as modern man is not the consumer, he is the trader. Our economic system is centered on the function of the market as determining the value of all commodities and as the regulator of each one's share in the social product. Neither force nor tradition, as in previous periods of history, nor fraud nor trickery, governs man's economic activities. He is free to produce and to sell; market day is judgment day for the success of his efforts. Not only commodities are offered and sold on the market; labor has become a commodity, sold on the labor market under the same conditions of fair competition. But the market system has reached out further than the economic sphere of commodities and labor. Man has transformed *himself* into a commodity, and experiences his life as capital to be invested profitably. If he succeeds in this, he is "successful" and his life has meaning; if not, he is a "failure." His "value" lies in his salability, not in his human qualities of love and reason or in his artistic capacities. Hence, his sense of his own value depends on extraneous factors: his success, the judgment of others. Hence, he is dependent on these others, and his security lies in conformity, in never being more than two feet away from the herd.

However, it is not only the market that determines modern man's character. Another factor, closely related to the market function, is the *mode* of industrial production. Enterprises become bigger and bigger; the number of people employed by these enterprises as workers or clerks grows incessantly; ownership is separated from management, and the industrial giants are governed by a professional bureaucracy interested mainly in the smooth functioning and the expansion of their enterprise rather than in the personal greed for profit *per se*.

What kind of man, then, does our society need in order to function smoothly? It needs men who cooperate easily in large groups, who want to consume more and more, and whose tastes are standardized and can be easily influenced and anticipated. It needs men who feel free and independent, not subject to any authority or principle or conscience, yet who are willing to be commanded, to do what is expected, to fit into the social machine without friction; men who can be guided without force, led without leaders, prompted without an aim—except the aim to be on the move, to function, to go forward.

This kind of man modern industrialism has succeeded in producing; he is the automaton, the alienated man. He is alienated in the sense that his actions and his own forces have become estranged from him; they stand above him and against him, and rule him rather than being ruled by him. His life forces have been transformed into things and institutions; and these things and institutions have become idols. They are experienced not as the result of his own efforts but as something apart from him, which he worships and to which he submits. Alienated man bows down before the works of his own hands. His idols represent his own life forces in an alienated form. Man experiences himself not as the active bearer of his own forces and riches but as an impoverished "thing," dependent on other things outside himself into which he has projected his living substance.

Man's social feelings are projected into the state. As a *citizen,* he is willing even to give his life for his fellow men; as a *private* individual, he is governed by egotistical concern with himself. Because he has made the state the embodiment of his own social feelings, he worships it and its symbols. He projects his sense of power, wisdom, and courage into his leaders, and he worships these leaders as his idols.

As a worker, clerk, or manager, modern man is even alienated from his work. The worker has become an economic atom that dances to the tune of automatized management. He has no part in planning the work process, no part in its outcome; he is seldom in touch with the whole product. The manager, who, on the other hand, is in touch with the whole product, is nevertheless alienated from it as something that is merely concrete, or useful. His aim is to employ profitably the capital invested by others; the commodity is merely the embodiment of capital, not something that, as an entity, matters to him. The manager has become a bureaucrat who handles things, figures, and human beings as mere objects of his activity. Their manipulation is called "concern with human relations," whereas the manager deals with the most *in*human relations—between automatons that have become abstractions.

Our consumption is equally alienated. It is determined by advertising slogans rather than by our real needs, our palates, our eyes, or our ears.

The meaninglessness and alienation of work result in a longing for complete laziness. Man hates his working life because it makes him feel a prisoner and a fraud. His ideal becomes absolute laziness—in which he does not have to make a move, where everything proceeds according to the Kodak slogan "You press the button; we do the rest."

This tendency is reinforced by the type of consumption necessary for the expansion of the market, leading to a principle that Aldous Huxley has very succinctly expressed in his *Brave New World* (1946). One of the slogans that everyone is conditioned with from childhood is: "Never put off till tomorrow the fun you can have today." If I do not postpone the satisfaction of my wish (and I am conditioned only to wish for what I can get), I have no conflict, no doubts; no decision has to be made; I am never alone with myself because I am always busy—either working or having fun. I have no need to be aware of myself as myself because I am constantly absorbed with consuming. I am a system of desires and satisfactions; I have to work in order to fulfill my desires—and these very desires are constantly stimulated and directed by the economic machine.

This alienated, isolated man is frightened. Not only because isolation and alienation in themselves produce anxiety, but also for a more specific reason. The bureaucratic industrial system, especially as it has developed in big corporations, produces anxiety, first of all because of the discrepancy between the bigness of the social entity (corporation, government, armed services) and the smallness of one individual. Furthermore, because of the general insecurity that this system produces in almost everybody.

Most people are employed and thus dependent on their bureaucratic bosses. They have sold not only their labor, but also their personality (their smiles, their tastes, even their friendships) in the bargain. They have betrayed their integrity, yet they can never be sure whether they will rise or fall, climb on the social ladder or be reduced to poverty, or at least to shame and embarrassment. In the midst of plenty, industrial bureaucratic society is a society of anxious and frightened men, men indeed so frightened about their possibilities of success or failure that they might be too frightened in these aspects of their personal life to be frightened about the possibility of total destruction by nuclear war.

Eventually, man in the most developed industrial societies becomes more and more enamoured of technical gadgets, rather than of living beings and processes of life. A new sports car, to many men, is more attractive than a woman. Interest in life and in the organic is replaced by interest in the technical and inorganic. The result is that man becomes indifferent to life and is even more proud of having invented missiles and nuclear weapons than he is abhorrent of them and saddened by contemplating the destruction of all life.

For the psychiatrist, certain consequences of this situation are important. Man, having been transformed into a thing, is anxious, without faith, without conviction, with little capacity for love. He escapes into empty busy-ness, alcoholism, extreme sexual promiscuity, and psychosomatic symptoms of all kinds, which can best be explained by the theory of stress. Paradoxically, the wealthiest societies turn out to be the sickest, and the progress of medicine in them is matched by a great increase of all forms of psychic and psychosomatic illness.

These considerations do not imply that industrialization, as such, is undesirable. On the contrary, without it the human race will not achieve the material basis for a dignified and meaningful human life. The question is: Which *form* should the industrial system have? That of bureaucratic industrialism, in which the individual becomes a small, insignificant cog in the social machinery, or that of a humanistic industrialism, in which alienation and the sense of impotence are overcome by the fact that the individual participates actively and responsibly in the economic and social process? A humanistic industrialism has many social and economic premises that I have no time to discuss. But one thing must be said: The aim of a humanist industrial society cannot be maximum profit for a few, or even maximum consumption for the many. Economic production must not become an end in itself, but only a means for a humanly richer life. It will exist in a society in which man *is* much, not one in which he *has* much or *uses* much. It must create the conditions for the productive man, not for the *homo consumens* or the *homo technicus,* or gadget man.

From all this follows a lesson for those countries now in transition from the feudal to industrial society. Indeed, they must become industrial societies, and fulfill the material needs of all their inhabitants. But they should be skeptical about the values existing in most advanced industrial societies, and not try to imitate them. Their aim should be to strive for a new form of society that is neither feudal nor industrial-bureaucratic; for a humanist industrialism, in which many of the human values of the past are realized, rather than remaining mere formulae or being swept away by the drunken wave of consumption. A revival of the spirit of enlightenment—ruthlessly critical, realistic, and cleansed from its overoptimistic, rationalistic prejudices, together with a revival of humanist values, not preached but realized in personal and social life—are the conditions for mental health and the survival of civilization.

· 3 ·

What I Do Not Like in Contemporary Society

Each year, beginning in 1967, Erich Fromm lived in Locarno, Switzerland, from April through September, until he changed his residency entirely from Mexico to Switzerland's Ticino in 1974. Contacts with the Italian press were soon made. Fromm wrote the following text for the Corriere della Sera, *the Milan evening newspaper, which published the text in January 1972. This text follows Fromm's English-language manuscript.*

There are so many things in contemporary society that I dislike that it is difficult to decide with which particular complaint to begin. But the fact is, it does not really matter, because it is quite clear that all the things I dislike are only various facets of the structure of modern industrial society; they form a syndrome, and all go back to the same root: the structure of industrial society, both in its capitalist and its Soviet form.

The first dislike I want to mention is the fact that everything and almost everybody is *for sale*. Not only commodities and services, but ideas, art, books, persons, convictions, a feeling, a smile—they all have been transformed into commodities. And so is the whole man, with all his faculties and potentialities.

From this follows something else: *Fewer and fewer people can be trusted*. Not necessarily do I mean this in the crude sense of dishonesty in business or underhandedness in personal relations, but in something that goes much deeper. Being for sale, how can one be trusted to be the same tomorrow as one is today? How do I know who he is, in whom I should put my trust? Just that he will not murder or rob me? This, indeed, is reassuring, but it is not much of a trust.

This is, of course, another way of saying that *ever fewer people have convictions*. By conviction I mean an opinion rooted in the person's character, in the total personality, and which therefore motivates action. I do not mean simply an idea that remains central and can be easily changed.

Another point is closely related to the former: The older generation tends to have a character that is very much shaped by the conventional patterns and by the need for successful adaptation. Many of the younger generation tend to have *no character at all*. By that I do not mean that they are dishonest; on the contrary, one of the few enjoyable things in the modern world is the honesty of a great part of the younger generation. What I mean is that they live, emotionally and intellectually speaking, from hand to mouth. They satisfy every need immediately, have little patience to learn, cannot easily endure frustration, and have no center within themselves, no sense of identity. They suffer from this and question themselves, their identity, and the meaning of life.

Some psychologists have made a virtue out of this lack of identity. They say that these young people have a "Protean character," striving for everything, not bound by anything. But this is only a more poetic way of speaking about the lack of self that B. F. Skinner's "human engineering," according to which man *is* what he is *conditioned to be*.

I dislike, too, the general *boredom* and *lack of joy*. Most people are bored because they are not interested in what they are doing, and our industrial system is not interested in having them be interested in their work. The hope for more amusement [than the older generation had] is supposed to be the only incentive that is necessary to compensate them for their boring work. But their leisure and amusement time, however, is boring. It is just as much managed by the amusement industry as working time is managed by the industrial plant. People look for pleasure and excitement, instead of joy; for power and property, instead of growth. They want to *have* much, and *use* much, instead of *being* much.

They are more attracted to *the dead and the mechanical* than to life and living processes. I have called this attraction to that which is not alive, using words of Miguel de Unamuno, "necrophilia," and the attraction to all that is alive, "biophilia." In spite of all the emphasis on pleasure, our society produces more and more necrophilia and less and less love of life. All this leads to great boredom, which is only superficially compensated by constantly changing stimuli. The less these stimuli permit a truly alive and active interest, the more frequently they have to be changed, since it is a biologically given fact that repeated "flat" stimuli soon become monotonous.

What I dislike most is summed up in the description in Greek mythology of the "Iron Race" the Greeks saw emerging. This description is—according to Hesiod's *Erga* (lines 132–42)—as follows: "As generations pass, they grow worse. A time will come when they have grown so wicked that they will worship power; might will be right to them and reverence for the good will cease to be. At last, when no man is angry anymore at wrongdoing or feels shame in the presence of the miserable, Zeus will destroy them too. And yet even then something might be done, if only the common people would rise and put down rulers who oppress them."

I cannot conclude without saying that, in spite of all this, I am not hopeless. We are in the midst of a process in which many people are beginning to give up their illusions, and, as Marx once said, to give up illusions is the condition for giving up circumstances that require illusions.

· 4 ·

The Disintegration of Societies

"La desintegración de las sociedades" was the title of the lecture that Fromm gave in January 1969 at a symposium of the Academia Nacional de Medicina in Mexico City. The topic of the symposium was "Understanding Death." The English-language version of this lecture manuscript was revised for publication by Fromm himself and was among his unpublished writings.

Speaking about the "disintegration of society" does not imply that society is an organism like a cell or the whole bodily system. Indeed, societies have been described in analogy with living organisms, for instance, by Oswald Spengler in his *Decline of the West* (1918–22), who said that in the sequence of birth, adolescence, maturity, and senescence societies pass through the same stages as the organism. However, while analogies may be stimulating, they do not prove anything.

Nevertheless, we can speak of the disintegration of societies without making such analogies if we understand a society as a system (or structure). The organism has it in common with society that they are both *systems,* and are subject to certain laws inherent in every system, even though the systems are very different in their substance. Such systems are, for instance, the human organism, the solar system, systems of language, ecological systems, political systems, systems of institutions, etc.

The Nature of Systems

The nature of a system is that all its parts are integrated in such a way that *the proper function of each part is necessary for the proper functioning of all other parts.* Thus, the system constitutes an entity different from the mere summation of all its components. From this fact the following features result:

(1) The system has a life of its own (regardless of whether it is an organism or an inorganic system), because it functions only as long as all its parts remain integrated in the particular form that the system demands. The system as a whole dominates the parts, and the parts are forced to function within the given system—or not at all. The system has an inner coherence that makes its change extremely difficult.

(2) If one tries to change one isolated part of the system, the change will not lead to a change of the system as a whole. On the contrary. The system will continue in its own way of functioning, absorbing the change of any given part in such a way that very soon the effects of the change are undone. A concrete example may serve: In the attempt to change the slums in big cities, it is often suggested that the most efficient way to do so is to build new, low-cost houses. One discovers, however, that after a while the new houses have turned into slums again, and the "slum system" continues to function as before. The

reason for this lies in the fact that if one only builds new houses without making fundamental changes in the entire system—educational, economic, psychological, etc.—the basic structure remains the same and hence reproduces the slum system, reducing eventually the newly built houses into *new* slums. A system can be changed only if, instead of changing only one single factor, real changes are made within the whole system so that a new integration of *all its parts* can take place.

(3) In order to understand which changes within the whole system are necessary and possible, the first condition is a proper analysis of the functioning of the system: a study of the causes for the dysfunctioning and the proper appreciation of the resources that are available for systemic changes.

(4) A general principle for the *optimal functioning* of a system or its *disintegration* can be formulated in the following way: A system can be considered to work efficiently when all its parts are properly integrated and work optimally with a minimum of energy—consuming friction among themselves and between the system and neighboring systems with which it is unavoidably in contact. One important condition for such proper functioning is that those parts of the system that are not adapted properly to new conditions outside the system are capable of responding regeneratively to these new conditions, and to adapt themselves to them. In contrast, disintegration of the system occurs when certain of its parts have lost the capacity for such adaptation, when they become ossified so that the friction within the system and the contradictions between the system and neighboring systems becomes so intense that eventually the system breaks up and disintegrates.

Between the two extremes, the optimal functioning of the system and its disintegration, are many shades of partial dysfunction. Whether a system can recover its balance or will disintegrate depends on the ability to introduce adequate changes based on the analysis of the system. It must be noted that there are systems such as the solar system, that operate entirely on the basis of physical laws outside human control. On the other hand, there are systems like that of the human organism or of a society which can be changed by human interference, provided this interference is based on the proper knowledge of the functioning of the system and the availability and of measures that permit systemic changes and have the willingness to do so.

(5) This does not mean that proper knowledge always can prevent the disintegration of the system. It is obvious that the human organism, at least up to now, is limited in its capacity for systemic change by the process of aging. In the same way, a society may not be able to make adaptive changes because it lacks the material basis for such changes, because, perhaps, there have been erosion of the soil, natural catastrophes, and so forth.

(6) However, very often systemic changes fail to occur, not because they would objectively be impossible, but for a number of *subjective* reasons. Perhaps, first of all, because of lack of comprehension of the functioning of the system and the reasons for its dysfunctioning. Secondly (in social systems), because special interests of groups within a society fight against changes that would be disadvantageous to them at the moment, although objectively speaking the refusal to give up certain privileges leads to the eventual destruction of such a class together with the rest of society. One last subjective difficulty is that most people, including many scientists, still think in terms of dated linear concept of cause and effect. They select the most obvious ills of a system and try to find *the* cause for these ills. They find it difficult to think in terms of processes within a system in which the understanding of one part makes it necessary to understand each other part; indeed, the understanding of the system requires much greater flexibility of thought. The understanding of society as a system is made particularly difficult by the fact that the thinking and feeling of the observer are, in themselves, parts of the system, and hence that the observer looks at the system not as it is truly functioning, but from the standpoint of his own wishes and of the part he plays in it.

On Disintegration of Social Systems

These general remarks about the nature of a "system" were necessary in order to speak now about the specific problem of the disintegration of societies. We must first remember what has been said already on the disintegration of systems: that systems disintegrate if contradictions within them become excessive, and if single parts and the system as a whole have lost the capacity for regenerative adaptation to changed circumstances. One more statement can be added to those made before: The process of disintegration of a society usually generates a great deal of violence and destructiveness within the disintegrating society (e.g., the period of the disintegration of the Roman Empire and of the disintegration of medieval society). The increasing violence today may be considered as an indication of disintegrating tendencies within the technological society.

We find in history a number of societies that have disintegrated in such a way that one might think of them as having died and been replaced by entirely new social systems. On the other hand, we find social systems in which such collapse was avoided and in which radical systemic changes led to the continuation of the system. One of the most frequently cited examples of the disintegration of a social system is the Roman Empire. Although the last word about the causes for the fall of the Roman Empire has not yet been spoken, there is a widespread acceptance of the idea that the reason for its disintegration is to be found in its incapacity to adapt itself to changing circumstances, particularly because it did not have the technological basis to solve the economic contradictions that had developed within the system. Thus, the mobile and cosmopolitan system of the Roman Empire was replaced by feudalism as it dominated Europe for about 1,000 years.

When we speak of the disintegration of a system, it does not mean that all its parts were simply destroyed. The individuals or their descendants in the system survived, together with a good deal of their knowledge and culture, and in fact when Europe moved from the Middle Ages to the Renaissance and the modern era, many of the building stones that had been created by the Greek and Roman societies were used in the construction of an entirely different system.

There are many other examples for such total disintegration of social systems. There are even many societies in which systemic change took place that permitted the radical reintegration of the older system. An obvious example for the latter case are the systemic changes that occurred within the capitalistic system between the beginning of the nineteenth century and the middle of the twentieth. These changes were due to a number of factors, especially the tremendous increase in productivity due to the application by ever more efficient machines and, lately, cybernetics and automation. Furthermore, the changes were part of the necessity for centralized big enterprises, which, again, were largely created by new technological capacities, the need to transform the worker into a customer, the social and political pressure of trade unions, and the need for more education among the population in order to make it fit to manage the ever more complicated machines.

Violent revolutions are not necessarily the proof for the disintegration of a system. All the conditions for nineteenth-century bourgeois society were already present before French Revolution, and the revolution only liberated society from the shackles that would have made further systemic changes impossible. We have some good examples in contemporary history for disintegration versus systemic changes of certain social and political systems. The system of the British Empire showed signs of a slow disintegration beginning with the end of the nineteenth century, in spite of the fact that Great Britain was victorious in the two great wars in the first half of the twentieth century. On the other hand, the system of German imperialism underwent certain changes but continued to develop in terms of its basic structure in spite of the fact that the nation was thoroughly beaten militarily and politically in the same two great wars.

Again, the study of the dysfunctioning of the British as against the continuing functioning of the German system (and we have to add the Japanese system) offer us excellent material for the understanding of the causes for disintegration versus those for adaptive reintegration of economic and political systems. So far, there are few studies of this kind, but no doubt they will be made and will greatly contribute to our understanding of the causes of the disintegration of social systems. One fact, however, is already clear, and that is that economic conditions are much more relevant than purely military ones, and that economic conquest and penetration is replacing the older forms of military conquest.

Disintegration or Reintegration of Contemporary Technological Society

Till now, we have spoken about the problem of reintegration versus disintegration of social systems in a purely theoretical way. But many of us are aware that this problem in the year 1969 is not merely a problem of theory: The serious question exists whether the Western social system is in the process of disintegration or whether a reintegration is possible. It is true that the Western social system seems to be at the height of its power: The development of theoretical thought has led to technical applications that appear to fulfill the dreams of past generations. Its capacity for material production on the basis of the new technology is increasing in an ever more rapid pace. The recent travel around the moon has been so enthusiastically greeted by the vast majority of the Western population because it seems to be a proof of the strength and efficiency of our system. Yet all these great successes of the Western system do not negate the fact that it is confronted with severe systemic dysfunctioning and the danger of disintegration. Let me mention briefly some of the contradictions that may result in the disintegration of our technological system.

The most important contradiction perhaps is the fact that the rich nations grow richer and the poor nations relatively poorer, and that no serious effort is being made to change this trend. Nothing shows this danger more drastically than the generally accepted prediction of experts that even now we must count upon large-scale famines in the underdeveloped world in the 1980s.

Another contradiction lies in the drastic split between the traditional religious and humanistic values that are still generally accepted in the Western world and new technological values and norms that are their very opposites. The traditional values say that one ought to do something because it is good, true, or beautiful, or, to put it differently, because it serves the unfolding and growth of man. The new technological value says one ought to do something because it is *technically possible*. If it is technically possible to travel to the moon, one ought to do it in spite of the fact that immensely more urgent tasks on earth are left undone. If it is technically possible to produce the most devastating weapons, one ought to do so regardless of the fact that these weapons threaten the whole of mankind with annihilation. The split between the conscious set of values that children are still taught and that a majority of adults still believe in and the *contradictory* set of values according to which adults act has the effect of wasting human energy, of creating a guilty conscience and a sense of purposelessness.

Another contradiction lies in the fact that whereas industrial society all over the world increases literacy, and eventually higher education, its educational progress is in sharp contrast to the inability of citizens for active critical thought. While on the one hand literacy increases, television creates a new type of illiteracy in which the consumer is fed by pictures, using his eyes and ears but not his brain. Briefly, while we are producing ever more efficient machines, man himself is losing some of his most important qualities. He becomes a passive consumer led by the big organization, which has no aim and vision except that of becoming ever bigger, more efficient, and growing faster.

The more powerful the person is over nature, the more powerless the man or woman is toward the machine. I want to give only a few examples to show that our total system finds itself in a state of serious disequilibrium, and that certain parts of it seem to have lost their adaptive and regenerative powers. This loss of adaptive function shows particularly clearly in our inability (1) to do away with nuclear weapons, and hence with the paralyzing threat of complete destruction, (2) to take measures for the overcoming of the increasing split between the poor and rich worlds, and (3) to take measures that give man control over the machine rather than to make him its servant.

The historical question with which we are confronted is whether Western society still has the vitality to make the necessary systemic changes in order to prevent disintegration, or whether we have lost control, and hence are headed for catastrophe. It seems to most observers that we still have the technical capacity for reintegration, and that our greatest weakness lies in the fact that we do not undertake an analysis of the system, and that particular interests take precedence over the interest in the reintegration of the system as a whole. There are some observers, like Jacques Ellul in France and Lewis Mumford in the United States, who have little hope that the process of disintegration can be stopped, although they do not exclude this possibility. There are many others accustomed to linear-cause-and-effect thinking, who believe that dealing with symptoms can stop the disintegration of the system; and there is a minority who believe that one has to destroy the system in order to construct a better one. (It appears that they do not see that such a destruction, at the very best, would lead to centuries of bloodshed and barbarization, and, given the present level of destructive forces, probably not only to the destruction of the present system but also the physical destruction of the larger part of mankind, if not of all life.)

It appears to me that the situation in which we find ourselves makes the study of the disintegration of systems, and particularly of social systems, not only one of the highest theoretical interest, but also one of vital necessity, if we are to survive. Never has human capacity for understanding of the critical and analytical thought been more necessary than today for the survival of the human race.

· 5 ·

The Search for a Humanistic Alternative

During the 1968 American presidential primary elections, the sixty-eight-year-old Fromm enthusiastically supported Eugene McCarthy, a candidate of the Democratic Party. (See also Fromm's newspaper advertisement "Why I Am for McCarthy" [E. Fromm, Ethik und Politik, pp. 256–60] and the election speech for Eugene McCarthy in Part II of the present volume.) Fromm saw in McCarthy the personification of humanism, a bearer of hope for a fundamental change in the history of humanity. Fromm himself gave many election speeches and traveled for months. In addition, he wrote an entire string of so-called memos, notes that he made available to McCarthy for his election campaign speeches and that McCarthy adopted—more or less unchanged—for these. The following election campaign speech was such a "memo," which Fromm wrote on March 16, 1968, one week before his sixty-eighth birthday. Thematically, it takes up the burning questions that Fromm discusses more thoroughly somewhat later in his book The Revolution of Hope *(1968). Particularly the concluding section of the speech shows how taken Fromm was with the mobilization of an alternative humanistic "movement," for which he at that time believed there was a broad basis in the American population. The shock caused by the election of the Republican, Nixon, might have to do with Fromm's not having, later, made himself a dynamo of such an alternative movement. In any case, it is certain that a severe heart attack suffered on December 7, 1966, which means before the course of the presidential candidates' campaign, made such an involvement impossible.*

Where Are We Moving to?

The dangers threatening the world and the United States with nuclear war, with a widening gap between poor and rich nations, by the decay of American cities, and by failure to change the situation of the "underdeveloped" segments of the American population are well known. It is recognized, furthermore, that in spite of this knowledge there is no plan, no effective action, to change the course that, if it is permitted to follow its own momentum, may lead to the collapse of civilization, or possibly to the total destruction of man.

Another fact is gaining recognition. I refer to the new social organization that is emerging in the most highly industrialized countries, especially the United States. This is the totally bureaucratized industrialism, that machine of which machines *and* men are parts, and which Lewis Mumford has called the "megamachine" (1967). The picture of today's society has been drawn by Aldous Huxley in *Brave New World* (1946) in novelistic fashion, by Mumford in a rich, penetrating cultural and social analysis, and, recently, although much more superficially, by Zbigniew Brzezinski (1968), who calls it the "technotronic society"; as well as dazzlingly but again only superficially by Herman Kahn in his recent *The Year 2000* (1967). In the new society of the second industrial revolution, described by these writers, the individual disappears. He becomes completely alienated. He is programmed by the principles of maximum production, maximum consumption, and minimal friction. He attempts to relieve his boredom by all kinds of consumption, including drugs and sex. This, and possibilities of neurologically and physiologically produced changes in his feelings, in addition to the manipulation of his thought processes by suggestive methods, will be used in the attempt to provide man's smooth functioning as a part of the megamachine.

This new society toward which we are moving constitutes a change in human existence in comparison to which the change from medieval to modern society is pale, and revolutionary changes like those resulting from the French and Russian revolutions appear like insignificant ripples of history.

What many of those who have accepted this development as unavoidable or as essentially beneficial do not see is the fact that man is not made to be a passive, unalive "thing," and that the state of chronic low-grade schizophrenia (separation of thought from effect) and depression that we see in their beginnings already now will either lead to outbursts of insane violence or to the dying out of such society because of lack of vitality.

What are the alternatives between which we can choose? The one still accepted by the majority—including men of goodwill and intelligence—is to let things go their way and to hope for the best. This alternative may avoid sleepless nights at present, but it will not change the course of the events that are moving toward a catastrophic development.

The second alternative is the one that might be called the "Maoist alternative" (although one cannot be sure whether those who believe themselves to be Maoists truly represent the thoughts and intentions of the Chinese leaders). This alternative proceeds from the premise that the system is moving toward catastrophe, and that no reform of any kind can change this course. The only chance for avoiding the catastrophe is a change of the system itself, and this change can occur only through revolution on an international scale, meaning that when all the underdeveloped countries turn against the industrial countries, and particularly their leader—the United States—they will be able to overthrow the system, just as the Chinese peasants over-threw their rulers in the cities.

That there is much logic and boldness in this second point of view cannot be denied. Yet it is one of despair, mixed with a good deal of romanticism, phraseology, and adventurism. A general attack against the United States would end in the estab-lishment of fascism within this nation and probably in all other industrialized countries, as well as in the most ruthless dictator-ships in the rest of the world. Should the Establishment of the United States see itself in serious danger, it would be forced into risking nuclear war, unless the Chinese themselves were to unleash such a war. But those advocating such a program forget that American society is not yet disintegrating, that many Americans, young and old, are not willing to be led on the path of destruction or of fascism. Furthermore, there exists nothing that could be called a "revolutionary" situation in the United States except in the romantic fantasies of a small number of people, and hence the application of revolutionary means in a non-revolutionary situation is, indeed, phraseology and adventurism.

Is there a third alternative? I believe there is. This possibility, slim as it is, may be offering itself for the last time at the present moment. It is an alternative that is real only as long as American society has not lost the basic elements of a democratic society, and as long as there are a considerable number of people who have not yet been emotionally emasculated, who have not yet become robots and organization-men.

The first question to be studied and discussed, if one speaks of a third alternative, is: How large a segment is the group, in America—among both young and old—who still have kept enough of the human substance, of the humanist and also the specifically American tradition, to be appealed to intellectually and emotionally? The question is: Are there a considerable number of Americans, ranging from conservatives to radicals, who can be "moved"—moved, in the double sense of the word: "touched" in their feelings and impelled to action? I do not claim to know the answer to this question of how large this segment of "movable" Americans is, and I do not think that anyone has the answer. From my own observation, however, I believe that there is a very good chance that this segment of America is considerable. It should also be noted that what matters here is not whether the segment has a clear awareness of the dangers and of alternatives. What matters is that they sense the truth and can be made aware of what they only sense dimly. The reason why awareness of the danger of the megamachine society could likely mobilize conservatives *and* radicals lies in the fact that the threat is so profound that it touches the vital interests of all those who are not yet completely alienated, and hence who can be alarmed by the threat.

The Conditions for a Humanist-Activist Alternative

The first condition is that people become *aware,* and that is something different from simply agreeing with the ideas they hear. To be aware means to wake up to something that one has felt or sensed without thinking it, and yet that one feels one has always known. It is a process that has a vitalizing and energizing effect because it is an active inner process and not the passive process of listening, agreeing, or contradicting.

Aside from the necessity of becoming aware, the awareness must refer to the system as a whole, and not to isolated and fractionated features. It is not enough to be aware that the war in Vietnam is senseless, dangerous and immoral; that Negro violence is a necessary outcome of the misery of black ghetto life; that more consumption, the use of more gadgets, does not increase happiness but only anaesthetizes the boredom. It is necessary to become aware that all these features are parts of a system that produces, inevitably, all these symptoms; to be aware that nothing is achieved if one fights isolated symptoms, but that one must change the system in which they are rooted.

That means becoming aware of the nature of an ever more totally bureaucratized industrial system guided by the goals of power, prestige, and pleasure, programmed by the principles of maximal production and minimal friction. It is necessary to become aware that this system as a whole dehumanizes man, and that man is no longer as he was in the nineteenth century—the ruler of his machines—but is ruled by them, the worker as well as the manager. Eventually, people must become aware that this system functions only with their consent and help, and that if they want to change it, it can be changed as long as democratic processes exist.

But it is not enough for people to become aware of the system. They must see *alternatives*. Indeed, one of the main obstacles to rational and adequate actions lies in the fact that people either see no alternatives to the status quo or they are presented with false and demagogic alternatives only in order to prove to them all the better that there are no real alternatives. One of these deceptive alternatives is the suggestion of returning to the pre-industrial age or of accepting the society of the megamachine. Another suggestion, in the political field, is that of allowing the collapse of the United States according to the domino theory or of pursuing the Vietnam War until the destruction of all Vietnam is achieved (and America has suffered severe material and moral losses).

Another deceptive alternative is that between the expropriation of all property or accepting the totalitarian, managerial society. Still another is that between theistic religion (Christianity) or soulless, idolatric materialism. The most fundamental of the erroneous alternatives is perhaps that between so-called "realism"—understood as automation uncontrolled by decisions based on human values—and utopianism, understood as unreal and unreliable goals, merely because they have not yet been realized.

The important task is to awaken people to the fact that there are true alternatives, that is to say, real possibilities that are neither the old nor its fictitious opposite. The real alternative in the field of social organization is that of a humanist industrialism: measures such as decentralization, self-management, individual responsible activity in all fields. This means not *expropriation* of property, but *control* of its administration guided by the principles of the optimum value for man's development. Legislation and constitutional amendments will probably suffice, but even constitutional changes could be part of the democratic process. (Cf. the Food and Drug Laws, the anti-monopoly laws, and many other interventions of the state in the field of "individual initiative.")

In the psycho-spiritual field there is the new alternative of a frame of reference that would be common to the theistic and the non-theistic person. In this frame of reference the goal of life is the fullest development of human powers, specifically those of reason and of love, including the transcending of the narrowness of one's ego and the development of the capacity to give oneself as well as a full affirmation of life and all that is alive as against the worship of the mechanical and dead. Eventually, the real alternative to realism and "utopia" results from the syndrome thought–knowledge–imagination–hope, which enables man to see the real possibilities, the seeds of which already exist in the present. If any single element of this syndrome is missing, no new alternatives are seen. The real alternative suggested here is that of radical changes brought about by using the democratic process and made possible by "moving" a large segment of the American people to act who prefer radical changes over today's physical and mental death.

The critique of the system toward which we are moving and the vision of new alternatives have been given in broad terms by quite a number of people who have occupied themselves with this problem. But what we know is not enough. Especially as far as the alternatives are concerned, a great number of studies and experiments are necessary in order to transform broad ideas into specific suggestions. This holds true for the questions of decentralization, of self-management, of the nature of rational versus irrational human needs, of incentives for work, of the problem of activity versus passivity, of a radical humanist philosophy, and many more problems. Among them, one of the foremost will be to decide whether the use of electronic computers, cybernation, automation, etc., needs to be curbed or modified so that man may regain his control over machines.

Once people begin to become aware of the fundamental problems, and to raise questions, they would challenge—and probably in many cases successfully—the best brains and the most devoted men and women in the various fields of the social and natural sciences, as well as in medicine, architecture, and city planning, to study the possibilities of humanistic alternative systems in a detailed and concrete form that would be in contrast with the alienated and mechanistic alternatives developed by Herman Kahn and others. The essential difference from the work of "think tanks" would be the premise that man is a central category in all planning and predictions. What characterizes Kahn's and other similar works is precisely that they deal with technical possibilities that are more or less predictable, but not with man as he is affected by these technical and social changes, and not with the changes in man that affect society. They ignore the value judgments man has to make in deciding whether he prefers maximal consumption and thus maximal alienation, or a lesser degree of consumption, that is, consumption as a means for a humanly richer life kept within dimensions that fit human reality. The alienated, quasi-schizophrenic style that has become the fashion with many social scientists necessarily means the elimination of man as a feeling, live, suffering, thinking human being in social analysis.

The Necessity for an Alternative Movement

But even if a considerable segment of the American people were "moved," even if this led to many studies provoked by a new interest in alternatives, this in itself would not be enough. It is a fact that even the best ideas and visions and programs do not in themselves have a lasting impact on man unless he is given a chance to act, to participate, and to share ideas and aims with others. If men are truly moved they will form the nucleus of a "movement" and this movement must permit them, in varying degrees, to cooperate in certain actions, to share feelings, ideas, and hopes, to make sacrifices, and to have to some extent common symbols or even rituals. An idea must be expressed in the flesh of group-feeling and -action in order to become effective. It can be demonstrated that ideas that have become influential were spread by small groups of enthusiastic adherents who impressed others by their enthusiasm and their way of living, by their ideas, and by the fact that the spirit of the idea found expression in the very way the groups constituted themselves and in the forms in which they functioned. (The Essenes, the early Christians, the monastic groups, the Society of Jesus, the Society of Friends, the Freemasons, and the early socialist and anarchist groups, are some examples of these.)

It is especially important for the intellectual to see that there is a need for shared action and feeling, which is greater in the young and in those who do not make intellectual or artistic pursuits their main occupation. Intellectuals are often so saturated with the problems they are working on that they feel little need for group life, and have not enough understanding for the great need of those who are seeking to find leadership and comradeship for meaningful action. The non-intellectuals' characteristic response to ideas is "that is all very good and true, but what can *I* do about it?" The intellectual knows what *he* can do: He thinks some more, writes another book, and perhaps lectures. But after all this is said and done, the student or the older person who does not participate actively in the intellectual process feels, and is, left alone. His question "What can *I* do about it?" really has a double meaning. One is "How can we change the system?" and the other is "What have you to suggest that *I* can *do* today?"

It is true that a small percentage of activist youth have found ways and means to "do something about it." Their action has consisted mainly in organizing and participating in protests, demonstrations, sit-ins, acts of civil disobedience, or active participation in the racist, feminist, or other struggles. Most of these activities are necessary and of great importance, but they are self-limiting because by their very nature of being mere protest they fail to attract sufficiently large numbers of people or to "move" that large sector of the American population that needs to be moved if there is to be a radical change.

I submit that people, young and old, who seriously believe in the need for an alternative should organize themselves in groups. The value of such groups is, in my opinion, splendidly demonstrated by Lewis Mumford's analysis of the historical function of small groups. He concludes, in *The Myth of the Machine* (1967): "Small seemingly helpless organizations that have an inner coherence and a mind of their own have in the long run often proved more effective in overcoming arbitrary power than the biggest military units—if only because they are so difficult to pin down and confront."

These groups should be relatively small, face-to-face groups of not more than a hundred members each. In order to avoid demagogic leadership and damaging ideology, there should be no central authority that controls the groups (in this respect, the Society of Friends is a good example). They must have a common idea—that of the search for the "humanist alternative"—and they should discuss the various possible roads to this end. They should overlap all political and religious creeds, and avoid making any particular conceptualization a condition for membership. It is of crucial importance that these groups should be different in principle from "discussion groups." The participants should oblige themselves to accept a certain conduct of life that demands sacrifice. Suggestions along this line would be that the members refrain from the satisfaction of unnecessary and alienating gadget needs, that they allot 10 percent of their income for purposes that further the aims of the movement, that they develop a new style of life—one of directness, truthfulness, and realism—that they give a certain amount of their time to study and to the active propagation of the aims of the movement among the people with whom they have social contact and with whom they work, and that they show objectivity and a lack of fanaticism as well as firmness and courage in all their behavior. This means, for instance, that today they would express their protest against the Vietnam War and the failure to change slum conditions (black and white) in an unequivocal way and in accordance with each person's conscience. Such groups should also have at least a minimum of common symbols and rituals. One may suggest that periods of shared silence and meditation would be among the groups' "ritual" expressions. The members should conduct their lives in a manner that would induce solidarity and the overcoming of fanaticism and egotism.

All these ideas are nothing but tentative suggestions. Working out a detailed and valid program for a group's life would be a matter of serious and prolonged discussion among those who want to participate. It is expected that these groups would form the active nucleus of a movement, and that they would attract a large number of people who are sympathetic to them and influenced by their dedication and seriousness as well as by the concrete suggestions and proposals emanating from the groups. Some older intellectuals should join the groups, but not as "leaders," and they should be as responsive to the situation of the young members as the latter should be to the older and more experienced ones.

· 6 ·

A New Humanism as a Condition for the One World

On April 4, 1962, Fromm gave a lecture entitled "A New Humanism as a Condition for the One World" in Sherwood Hall in La Jolla, California. The lecture existed as transcript of the tape as well as in manuscript form among his unpublished writings.

There is no doubt that one world is coming into existence. Probably this is the most revolutionary event in the history of mankind. One world has come into existence, as we can see already, in the sense that industrial production eventually will be common to all peoples of the world and will create a certain closeness between all peoples, greatly enhanced by our new methods of communication. But the question is: whether this one world will come into existence as a livable world or whether it will end as one great battlefield.

The question indeed is: Is modern man, the man of the twentieth century, really prepared to live in one world? Or is it that we are intellectually living in the twentieth century and emotionally living in the stone age? Is it that while we are preparing this one world our feelings and goals are still those of tribalism? And by tribalism I mean, in fact, an attitude that we find in most all primitive tribes: one has confidence only in the members of one's own tribe, one feels a moral obligation only to the members of one's own tribe, to the people—and this is very essential, although it sounds trivial—an obligation only to those who have eaten the same food, sung the same songs, and spoken the same language. In this tribalism the stranger is considered with suspicion, and projections of all the evil in oneself are made upon this stranger. Morality, in fact, in tribalism, is always an interior morality, valid only for the members of the same tribe; and it doesn't make the slightest difference, humanly speaking, whether this tribe is one of a hundred people or a thousand people or five hundred million people. It is always the same: that the stranger, one who does not belong to the same tribe, is not experienced as a full human being.

We find ourselves in the midst of tribalism. We call it *nationalism*. We, indeed, seem to salute it as the great liberation of nations from former dependence on stronger nations—which in some way of course is true. But at the same time we also see that the nationalism that started in the Western World really only a hundred and fifty years ago as a result of the French Revolution has now become the mode of feeling of almost the entire world. I feel that this is a very dangerous development, in view of the fact that unless man learns to live as *one* man, a part of *one* world, this nationalism will cause conditions and situations in which he is in danger of destroying himself. Unless we develop a new humanism, there will *be* no *one* world.

The History of the Idea of Humanism

When I say a "new humanism" I don't mean really that there is anything new. Humanism, as a philosophy, is about 2,500 years old. There's nothing new in it except that it is new for us. We have forgotten humanism for the last fifty years. So let me try to remind you of the history of the idea of humanism in our tradition. I would have to talk about a Chinese and Indian humanism expressed in Taoism and Buddhism, but this would take a little too much time, so I might as well begin with the idea of humanism in the Old Testament.

One expression of humanism in the Old Testament is that God creates only *one* man. And as Talmudic sources say, God created one man only in order to indicate two things: first, that no man can say, "I am superior to you because my ancestors were superior to yours," and second, to indicate that anyone who destroys one single life is as if he had destroyed mankind. Another expression of the idea of humanism, of the *one* man, is the statement in the Old Testament that man is created in the likeness of God: that all men, hence, are equal, are the same in spite of the fact that they are not the same, because of their all being created in the likeness of God. And eventually you find in the Old Testament a command of love that is very significant and often overlooked and neglected, one that refers not only to the love of our neighbor but that refers to the love of the stranger.

The stranger is precisely the person with whom we are not familiar. The stranger is precisely the person who does not belong to the same tribe or to the same nation or to the same culture, and the Bible says: "Love the stranger, for you have been strangers in Egypt and hence you know the soul of the stranger" (Lev. 19:33). Indeed, only if one has experienced that which the stranger experiences, if one can put oneself in his place, one can understand him, or to put it more broadly, only if one can experience what any other human being experiences can one understand him, can one know what he feels.

Eventually you have perhaps the most explicit expression of Old Testament humanism in the prophetic concept of messianism. There the concept of tribalism is overcome in a vision of all nations being the same favorites of God and not any one nation being the favorite. Let me read you a sentence from Isaiah: "In that day," he says (Is. 19:23–25), "shall there be a highway out of Egypt to Assyria [the traditional two enemies of the Hebrews at that time] and the Assyrian shall come into Egypt and the Egyptian into Assyria and the Egyptians shall serve with the Assyrians. In that day shall Israel be the third with Egypt and with Assyria, a blessing in the midst of the land. Whom the Lord of hosts shall bless saying, Blessed be Egypt my people and Assyria the work of my hands, and Israel mine heritance."

This same humanistic tradition is continued in the New Testament. There the command is "Love thine enemy" (Mat. 5:44), and indeed between loving the enemy and loving the stranger there is very little difference, because if I love the enemy the enemy ceases to be a stranger, he becomes my neighbor, he becomes I and, hence, he really ceases to be an enemy. "Love thine enemy" is a paradox, but a paradox only because, in reality, once I love the stranger and the enemy, there is no more enemy.

Of course we know that the Catholic Church was founded on the basis of humanism and universalism, as against national boundaries. In the humanism of the late Middle Ages, a great Christian thinker like Nicholas of Cusa said that the humanity of Christ is binding man in the world and that it is the highest proof of the inner unity of mankind. His version of humanism was precisely that Christ's humanity is a guarantee for the oneness of all men.

The idea of humanism also has its roots in the Greek and Roman tradition. In Sophocles' drama *Antigone,* the heroine was fighting against what we would perhaps call today a fascist emperor, Creon, because she insisted that the law of nature—

which is a law of compassion for men—has precedence over the law of the state, and she is willing to die in order to fulfill the law of humanity when this law of humanity is contradicted by the law of the state. And so she buries her brother in spite of the fact that he was a traitor against the state.

The concept of humanism is expressed not only in Greek *thinking*, in Sophocles' *Antigone*, but also in Greek and Roman philosophy—especially in the concept of natural law, a law rooted in the nature of man and which has precedence over all other man-made, especially state, laws. One sentence from *Antigone* expresses the idea of natural law very beautifully. She says: "Not of today and yesterday is this the law, but ever has it life and no man knows whence it came and how."

You have in the thought of Cicero perhaps the most potent formulation of the natural-law idea, and this thinking of Cicero's entered Christian thought in the Middle Ages and became very powerful, very potent, in the development of Christian thought. Let me just read you one statement by Cicero: "You must now conceive of this whole universe as one commonwealth, of which both gods and men are members." Now, you see, here you have the concept of one commonwealth of all men: not a League of Nations, not a commonwealth of nations, but a commonwealth of men, in which every man has his loyalty to mankind and, as Cicero says very beautifully, ". . . of which both gods and men are members."

It would take too much time to talk about the development of the humanistic idea in the Late Middle Ages, in Thomas Aquinas. I should just like to mention that the idea of natural rights, which you find later on in the eighteenth century and which you find especially in the development of American thought and in the American concept of human rights, is a sequence to the development of natural law as it was developed in both the Greco-Roman and the Judaeo-Christian traditions.

The humanist idea in the Renaissance was one of "humanity," or *humanitas* in Latin (which is characteristic of all modern thought from the Renaissance on), in a mostly nontheological concept. Nevertheless, it was an idea of humanity that was a direct continuation of Greco-Roman and Judaeo-Christian religious tradition. In this specifically Renaissance concept, man is interpreted in his natural "suchness." Man is as he is and the task given to man is to unfold fully. The ideal of the Renaissance man is a universal man, the many-sided, all rounded realization of humanity within each individual. Each individual is the bearer of all humanity and the task of man is to unfold the humanity within himself.

This Renaissance thinking is then followed by the thinking that is probably the height of humanism in the Western tradition: the thinking of the eighteenth-century, or Enlightenment, philosophers.[1]

The humanist thought of the eighteenth century had a concept of man in general, of the essence of man. Now, if we speak of "essence" and stay in the tradition of philosophical terminology, we mean by "essence," briefly, that by the virtue of which a thing is what it is. So if we speak of the essence of man, we speak of that by the virtue of which man is human. Is there such a thing? Today many, if not most, social scientists are prone to believe that while this is true biologically and anatomically (it can hardly be denied), it is not really true psychologically. There are many social scientists who believe that man is born as an empty piece of paper, on which culture or society writes its text. Certainly the philosophers of the eighteenth century did not believe that. They believed that there is such a thing as human nature, a human constitution, more than in simply an anatomical or physiological sense. The philosophers of the eighteenth century elucidated a difference that I believe is very valid today, as it was then, a difference between

---

1. Cf., especially, E. Cassirer, 1932, and C. L. Becker, 1946; in E. Fromm, 1961, I wrote on the topic of how humanist philosophy is continued in socialist humanism.

this "essence" of man, between human nature as we find it in general, and the specific form in which human nature is expressed in each society and each culture. In other words, we never see human nature as such, we never see man in general, but we can infer from the many manifestations of man in various cultures and in various individuals what that is which man has in common: what that is which is specifically human.

Jean-Jacques Rousseau expressed the same idea, but he made one point that quite a few years later was taken up by Freud again: He pointed to the contradiction between the natural inclinations of man and the demands of society. This was a very important point to make. As I said, Freud made it later in a more specific form pointing to the conflict between sexual demands and the mores of society, and Freud assumed that neurosis actually developed out of this conflict. Well, I'm not so sure that he was right in this specific assumption, but nevertheless Freud's assumption had a much more *general* validity and meaning, namely, of pointing precisely to that which Rousseau had pointed out: the contradiction between social demands and the demands, let us say, of humanity within man. Let me remind you that John Locke presented a theory postulating that in order to understand what government ought to be, one had only to consult the nature of man. Locke's theory became very potent in the American tradition because of its influence on Jefferson and others.

I should like to quote a concept by one of the most significant philosophers who wrote about humanism, the German philosopher Johann Gottfried von Herder (1744–1803). For him, man, in contrast to the animal, was born feeble and needed to develop in himself humanity: "The artificial instinct of reason, humanity, and the human mode of living—the specifically human—is the highest flowering of natural evolution." Herder inherited the same concept, that man as an animal is the weakest, most helpless, and most incomplete of all animals; but that he has reason, however, that which is specifically human, and in the development of this specifically human quality he becomes the highest product of natural evolution.

The ideas of Gotthold Ephraim Lessing (1729–1781), another great humanist, went in a similar direction. He considered it the task of man to realize the essence of the human species. You see in Lessing's works the same concept, namely that that which is specifically human—the essence of man, the essence of humanity—must be realized, must be made manifest, must be developed. This is the task of man. And it's quite an irony of history that Lessing spoke of the Third Reich a little over a hundred years before Hitler, as that Reich in which humanity would reach its perfection, in which all human contradictions would be overcome in a new oneness and a new harmony of man.[2]

The most important of all humanist thinkers of the eighteenth and nineteenth centuries was perhaps Johann Wolfgang von Goethe. I should like to mention a few ideas of Goethe here. One that he expressed, very similar to those of Nicholas of Cusa, as well as those of Herder and Lessing, was the idea that man carries in himself not only his own individuality but all humanity with all its potentialities, although man, because of the limitations of his existence, can realize only part of these potentialities. The goal of life, to Goethe, was to develop through individuality to universality. I should like to stress this, because eighteenth-century thinking up to the philosophy of Goethe (and later of Marx) was a thinking in which one did not believe that one reached universality by diminishing individuality, by making himself like everyone else in order to feel his one-ness with others. On the contrary, it was believed that man, only by developing his own individuality fully, could come to the experience of his own humanity—and that means of all humanity. He would feel one with all, then, precisely because

---

2. Fromm is here referring to claims that Hitler would make concerning the Germans of the 1930s.

he had become fully himself. And if he does not become fully himself, if he remains, mentally speaking, a stillborn person, then he will neither have nor be able to feel that humanity which he carries within himself.

Perhaps the greatest, most significant expression of Goethe's humanism, and one that is very important for our day, is expressed in a drama that has been translated into English, although I don't think it's available any longer in print. It's the drama *Iphigenia*. Now, there was a Greek drama *Iphigenia*, written by Euripides. The story is briefly this: Iphigenia, the daughter of Agamemnon, was to be sacrificed to the gods in order to obtain favorable winds for the Greek ships (bound for Troy), but a merciful goddess carries her away before she is killed to an island of barbarians where a King Thoas rules, and he is convinced by her to end a custom that he had insisted on up until this time, namely, to kill every stranger who was stranded on his island. This barbaric habit may sound strange to us, but truly we shouldn't be so surprised: The stranger was, as I have said before, the person outside the tribe, hence the person who was not experienced as being fully human in the same sense in which we experience those close to us. It happens that King Thoas makes Iphigenia the priestess of the temple of Artemis. He is kind to her. He trusts her. But one day her brother Orestes comes, with a friend. The three propose to escape, to flee, to go back to Greece without the knowledge of the king— and to steal the idol of Artemis. In the Greek drama, after some difficulties they succeed.

In the drama by Goethe they have the same plan and at first Iphigenia agrees, but after she has agreed she changes her mind because she feels that she cannot betray the king who had confidence in her. She is actually confronted with what we call today "two evils," the greater evil to be killed herself and to have her brother and his friend killed, the lesser evil to betray the king. Now, usually today we are prone to believe that if we have to choose between two evils we should choose the lesser evil and we forget that in choosing the lesser, we generally only postpone the time until the bigger evil eventually occurs—with even more certainty.

Iphigenia refuses to choose between the two evils and she proposes that there are not necessarily only the two alternatives but might be a third, a third possibility: the possibility of being human. That means to tell the truth to the king, to act fully as a human being, risking the possibility that he might kill her and avoiding the two other evils, which, from a moral standpoint, are both unacceptable. She tells the truth to the king and the king answers:

> *And dost thou think that*
> *The uncultured Scythian will attend*
> *The voice of Truth and Humanity*
> *Which Arteus the Greek heard not?*

Iphigenia answers:

> *This voice is heard by everyone,*
> *Born beneath whatever clime,*
> *Within whose bosom flows the stream of life*
> *Pure arid unhindered.*

And, indeed, in Goethe's drama the king is touched by the voice of truth and humanity and he sends Iphigenia and her brother and his friend away to their homeland. This drama of Goethe's is important because here is the reliance on the voice of humanity as the one solution that can save man when it seems he is confronted only with the various forces of evil. I believe that this solution of Goethe's has some significance for our time. We seem to be caught in various alternatives that, although using different names, are all alternatives of destruction. I believe that it is very important to recognize that if we take the humanist tradition of our culture seriously, then indeed we must consider whether there are not other possibilities outside the cliché alternatives, and whether the most important possibility is not the one of humanity and of truth.

Goethe was also—and it is not unimportant to mention this too—a humanist in that he was an anti-nationalist. He lived a long life, as you know, and toward the end of it that nationalism had taken over not only in France but was beginning to do so in Germany. It was an idea rampant in the wars between Napoleon and the Germans, wars that the Germans called "the wars of liberation." Goethe was certainly one of the greatest *Germans,* but I want to read you a few things he said that counter this. He said in 1814—when Napoleon was already beaten by the victorious German liberation army—that the German nation was nothing, but that the individual German was something; and yet the world imagined the opposite to be true. The Germans should be dispersed throughout the world, Goethe believed, like the Jews, in order fully to develop all the good that is in them for the benefit of mankind. In a letter dated much earlier [March 15, 1799, to Johann Jakob Hottinger], he wrote: "At a time when everyone is busy creating new Fatherlands, the Fatherland of the man who thinks without prejudice and can rise above his time is nowhere and everywhere." . . .

You can see here how Goethe was opposing the new wave of nationalism that was the very negation of the humanism which had been growing and unfolding in Western culture, one might say, from the thirteenth century through the eighteenth. Goethe was the last of the tradition of humanists in the nineteenth century. Then began the new wave of nationalism, and it is one of those ironies of history that the French Revolution, was based on and stimulated by a philosophy that was essentially humanistic, was precisely the revolution that created the new nationalism, which began to create the new idol, the national state. In the national state, nationalism was combined with the industrial revolution as representing powerful economic interests. Force and nationalistic sentiments were used in order to realize the powerful economic interests that existed within that national state.

This nationalism, which began in the French Revolution and in the German-French Wars, spread rampant into Germany after 1871, when Germany was finally united. We find it even more rampant later in Germany, as well as in Stalinist Russia and in today's Russia, the Soviet Union. It found its terrifying expression in two world wars; it is equally terrifying as the cause for a possible third and, this time, nuclear war.

I should like to read you something from a man who, in his personal life, represented this change from humanism to nationalism and who expressed it in the most sensitive fashion. He is a Belgian poet, Émile Verhaeren, who was a pacifist, a humanist, and a socialist before 1914 and who changed under the impression of the war, as many other men changed. He wrote, in a book that he dedicated to himself, the following lines: "He who writes this book in which hate is not hidden was formerly a pacifist. For him no disillusionment was ever greater or more sudden. It struck him with such violence that he thought himself no longer the same man, and yet it seems to him that in this state of hatred his conscience became diminished. He dedicates these pages, with emotion, to the man he used to be." Now, this is perhaps the most illuminating expression of a change, in one person, that in reality can be seen as the change in the culture and social climate between two centuries, between eighteenth-century humanism and nineteenth- and twentieth-century nationalism.

I should like to mention briefly that the most important expression of eighteenth-century humanism in the nineteenth century is to be found in Socialist thought of various types—perhaps most clearly in the thought of Marx. Now this may sound surprising to you, because most of you have heard that Marx was materialistic, that he believed that the main motivation of man was material, and so on. Actually Marx is much quoted and little understood, but so is the Bible. Unfortunately, the most important text of Marx on the concept of man—his most important philosophical text—was not even translated into English until a year ago. But one doesn't need to read it in order to understand that Marx's philosophy was a straight continuation of Spinoza, Hegel, and Goethe and that the kind of so-called Marxism which the Soviet Union claims to have has as much to do with Marx, as, let us say, the Renaissance Popes have to do with the teachings of Christ.

I should like to read you one or two quotations in order at least to make what I say sound less absurd. Marx's aim for man was precisely like that of Spinoza, like that of Goethe: the independent man, the free man: "A being does not regard himself as independent unless he is his own master, and he is only his own master when he owes his *existence* to himself. A man who lives by the favor of another considers himself a dependent being."[3] Man is independent only if he "appropriates his manifold being in an all-inclusive way and thus as a whole man." This latter concept of the "whole man" comes from the Renaissance through Spinoza, Leibniz, and Goethe to Marx. Further: "All his *human* relations to the world—seeing, hearing, smelling, tasting, touching, thinking, observing, feeling, desiring, acting, loving—in short, all the organs of his individuality . . . are . . . the appropriation of *human* reality. . . . Private property has made us so stupid and partial that an object is only *ours* when we have it, when it exists for us as capital or when it is directly eaten, drunk, worn, inhabited, etc., in short, *utilized* in some way. . . . Thus, *all* the physical and intellectual senses have been replaced by the simple alienation of *all* these senses: the sense of *having*. The human being had to be reduced to this absolute poverty in order to be able to give birth to all his inner wealth."

Another statement of Marx is very characteristic for all humanistic thinking; the statement concerns man as an active be-

---

3. Karl Marx, "Economic and Philosophical Manuscripts," quoted in E. Fromm, *Marx's Concept of Man*, p. 138.

ing as against a passive being. This statement refers particularly to love. For Marx, as for Spinoza, the problem is never "to be loved," as it is for most of us, and the question is never the principal question, "How does anyone love us?" but the problem is our capacity *to* love and the quality of love as an *active* quality. "If you love without evoking love in return, that is, if you are not able by the *manifestation* of yourself as a loving person to make yourself a *beloved* person, then your love is impotent, a misfortune"[4]

The Relevance of Humanism for Today

Now I should like to discuss two aspects of humanism that are important for ourselves. One is, if you please, a scientific aspect, namely: Is there such a thing as the "essence of man"? The eighteenth century was rather optimistic about the essence of man. The general picture in that century was that man is reasonable, good, and easily directed or influenced in the direction of the good. Today some people like Reinhold Niebuhr and others assure us that it is almost sinful to have such a naive belief, a belief in the goodness of man. But I don't believe we need such exhortations: The period we have lived through and are living through gives us sufficient proof of the irrationality and even insanity of man that we don't really need to be reminded of how evil man can be. The question is, and I think the essential question for the science of man to discover is: What is the essence of man? What is that that can objectively be described as human?

In my book *The Sane Society* (1955), I have tried to discuss this question. Here I only want to stress that the essence of man is not a substance, that it isn't that man is good or man is bad, but that there is an essence that remains the same throughout history. The essence of man is a constellation or, as Heideg-

---

4. Ibid., p. 168.

ger calls it, a configuration—a basic configuration. And as I see it, this configuration is precisely one of an existential dichotomy or, to use somewhat less technical language, it is precisely one of a contradiction between man as an animal who is within nature and between man as the only thing in nature that has awareness of itself. Hence, man can be aware of his separateness and lostness and weakness. Hence, man has to find new ways of union with nature and with his fellow man. Man was born, historically and individually, and, when he becomes aware of his separateness from the world, he would become insane unless he found a method to overcome this separateness and find union. This is, I am sure, the strongest passion in man: to avoid and overcome the full experience of separateness and to find a new union.

The history of religion, and the history of man in general (and of individuals, too) show, that there are two ways of overcoming separateness and of achieving union. The one you will find in all primitive religions, and it is a way to return to nature, to make man again into a pre-human animal, as it were, and to eliminate that in man which is specifically human: his reason, his awareness. This elimination is done in all sorts of ways: by drugs, by orgies, or simply by identification with animals, by putting oneself in the state of an animal—especially in the state of, say, a bear, a lion, or a wolf. In other words, it is the attempt to overcome the sense of separateness by ceasing to be human and by regressing, if you please, to the natural state in which man is a part of nature and in which he might become an animal. But, as the Bible expresses it symbolically, once Adam and Eve have left the Paradise—that is, that state of oneness in which man is not yet born as man—two angels with fiery swords watch the entrance and man cannot return.

Mankind's other solution to overcoming separateness and gaining union seems to have been found in the period between 1500 B.C. and 500 B.C. in China, India, Egypt, Palestine, and Greece: Man found oneness not by regressing but by developing his specifically human powers of reason and of love to such an extent that the world became his home; by becoming fully human he lived in a new harmony with himself, with his fellow men, and even with nature. This was the idea of prophetic messianism. It was also the idea of late-medieval religious thought. And it was the idea of eighteenth-century humanism. In fact, it is still the essence of religious and spiritual thought of the Western tradition: Man's task is to develop his humanity, and in the development of this humanity he will find a new harmony and hence the only way in which he can solve the problem of being born.

Being born, we are all asked a question and we have to give an answer—not one with our mind and our brain, but, every moment, one with our whole person. There are only really two answers. One answer is to regress and one answer is to develop our humanity. And there are many people—and I suppose these days *most* people—who try to avoid the answer and who fill the time with all the many things that we call entertainment or diversion or leisure time or whatever it may be. But I believe we find ultimately that this solution is no solution, that the people who choose it are all bored and depressed, except that they are not aware of this.

I spoke briefly about my own concept of how one could conceptualize the basic constitution of man in terms of constellation rather than in terms of a substance, but of course this topic would require many hours in order to develop, and certainly I shall not try.[5] Here I only want to add one other thought: The essence of man will become important only to those to whom, and only at a time when, the experience of the oneness of man is alive again. Today it is not alive.

---

5. See E. Fromm, *Man for Himself: An Inquiry into the Psychology of Ethics*, pp. 38–50; *The Sane Society*, pp. 22–66; and especially E. Fromm and Ramón Xirau, eds., *The Nature of Man*, pp.3–23.

* * *

What, then, is this experience of humanism? With the above survey I have tried to show you that the experience of humanism is that—as Terence expressed it—"Nothing human is alien to me"; that I carry within myself all of humanity; that, in spite of the fact that there are no two individuals who are the same, the paradox exists that we all share in the same substance, in the same quality; that nothing which exists in any human being does not exist in myself. I am the criminal and I am the saint. I am the child and I am the adult. I am the man who lived a hundred thousand years ago and I am the man who, provided we don't destroy the human race, will live a hundred thousand years from now.

This proposition has a very significant connection with one phenomenon with which it is usually not connected, namely, the phenomenon of the unconscious. Freud was not the first who discovered the unconscious, but he certainly was the first to give it a full systematic exploration. Nevertheless, his concept of the unconscious was still a very limited one. He thought that certain instinctual desires, such as incestuous desires or murderous desires, were repressed. Well, they are. But the problem is a wider one: What is really our consciousness? Our consciousness is all those human experiences of which our particular society permits us to be aware. Usually, aside from very small individual differences, we are aware only of that which our language, our logic, and the taboos of our societies permit us to be aware. There is, you might say, something like a "social filter," and only those experiences that can pass through that social filter are the things we are aware of; they are our consciousness.

And what is our unconscious? Our unconscious is humanity. Our unconscious is the universal man. Our unconscious is all that is human—the good and the bad—all that exists in everybody, *minus* that small sector which is conscious, which represents the experience, thinking, feeling of the culture that we are thrown into rather accidentally. Our unconscious is the *total* man, and hence the great significance of being in touch with our unconscious is not to discover our incestuous desires, or this, that, and the other (which may sometimes not be unimportant). The great importance of the Freudian discovery of the possibility of being in touch with our unconscious is, precisely, that if we are in touch with it, then we are in touch with humanity; then we are in touch with the total man in us; and then, indeed, there is no more stranger. Further, there is no more judging of others in the sense that we consider ourselves superior to them. If we are in touch with our unconscious, then, indeed, we experience ourselves as we experience everybody else. Indeed, we overcome that separation within ourselves in which we are aware only of that which is expressed in our particular tribe or culture, and we get in touch with that which we share with all humanity.

Nationalism as well as tribalism are precisely the opposite. There we are not in touch with humanity. We are only in touch with one sector of humanity and we perform a very simple operation: we project all the evil in us on the stranger, and hence the result is that he is a devil and we are the angels. That is what we experience in all wars, what is experienced in fights between people in their personal lives, and that is what we have experienced on both sides in the cold war, too. I believe that man is indeed forced today to choose between a renewal of humanism—of taking seriously the spiritual foundation of our Western culture, which is a foundation of humanism or—having no future at all.

It was, if I could quote him once more, Goethe who said: "There is only one important difference between various historical periods, namely, that between periods which have faith and periods which do not have faith. Those who have faith flourish and are alive, and those who do not have faith decay and eventually die." The thirteenth century and the eighteenth century were undoubtedly periods of faith. I am afraid that ours in the West is a period of a great lack of faith, that actually the hate we find so rampant more and more in the Western World and the United States is only an expression that people do not love and in fact that they do not know what they live for. Certainly, the hate is an expression of moral despair and of a moral defeatism. If one has to affirm one's culture by trying to save it by war, one will neither save one's values nor even one's life, as things are today.

I believe we still have the choice of whether we can renew the very roots of our tradition, which is the Greek-Roman, Judaeo-Christian tradition of humanism. If we are able to take those values seriously, values about which we talk all the time, then indeed there might come a new vitality to our culture and we might have a future. If we are not able to renew our roots, then whatever we say and whatever our weapons are, the West will not survive. I think we are confronted basically with a decision which is a *fundamental* decision. It is very beautifully expressed in the Old Testament: "I put before you today Life and Death, Blessing and Curse, and you choose Life" [Deuteronomy 30:19]. I believe what man today *has* to choose, in a world that is becoming One World, is precisely Life—and that means a new experience of humanisn. If he cannot choose that, he will not, I am afraid, manage the new "One World."

· PART II ·

Humanistic Initiatives and Confessions

· 7 ·

The Idea of a
World Conference

The "Remarks Concerning the Suggestion for a Papal Conference
on the Solution of Current Dangers to the Survival of Humanity"
(as Fromm called the matter in the following initiative, written first
as a letter in 1966) were among Fromm's unpublished writings.
They offer persuasive evidence of his concern with, involvement in,
and wealth of ideas relating to the discovery of answers to humanity's
crisis situation during the middle of the Cold War. In one of the
letters accompanying the "Remarks," Fromm adds that he was "sud-
denly hit by the thought" and that "the attempt is what matters."

That this harsh critic of any religious institution would want to
involve the Pope of the Catholic Church in a conference on world
peace has to do, on the one hand, with the lasting impression made
on Fromm by the basic humanistic stance of Pope John XXIII (1958–
63) and, on the other hand, with the increased prestige of the Catholic Church in the world after the reforms of Vatican Council II
(1962–65) and with the Council's opening of the Church for en-
gagement in the world. Documents among the unpublished writings
do not establish what particular effects Fromm's letter had. Nevertheless, the correspondence makes it apparent that his initiatives re-
sounded positively with Senator Fulbright, Harvey Cox, James
Luther Adams, George Williams, Louis Sohn, Lewis Mumford,

Marcus Raskin, Stewart Meacham, Norman Cousins (of the Saturday Review, *who acquainted the Pope with the idea), Gilbert White, Alfred Hassler, Father Thomas Merton, Gunnar Jahn, Archbishop Angelo Dell'Acqua, Mihailo Markovic, Adam Schaff, and others.*

It must have been all the more disappointing to Fromm that the Pope and the Catholic Church could not be moved. Just three months later, Fromm writes in a letter to Clara Urquhart: "We will have to accept the fact that the Pope will do nothing."

An analysis of the present situation has led most thoughtful and informed people to the conviction that the escalation of the war in Vietnam is leading to an ever-increasing possibility of nuclear war on a worldwide scale, which would result in the destruction of the larger part of the human race and of the spiritual values that have governed, or at least have guided, man for several thousand years. Serious attempts are being made on many sides—religious, pacifist, humanist, purely political—to stem the tide. The activity of ad hoc organizations, the publication of books, articles, and appeals increase steadily. Perhaps never before in history have so many different individuals and groups taken upon themselves the responsibility of responding to a common danger, and yet they are often aware of a sense of futility, seeing that their efforts do not bring about any change. It appears that their efforts are like those of the Greek chorus, which foresees the tragedy and yet is powerless to prevent it.

But even the danger of thermonuclear war is not the only threat to man today. Because of new technology, all previous methods of production and modes of consumption are changing. The independent man—the man who makes his own decisions and relies on his own conscience—is being replaced by the organization man, who takes and gives orders. The poor peoples of the world demand their share in the goods created by human inventiveness, and will no longer wait; meanwhile, in spite of many efforts, the rich nations grow richer and the poor ones grow poorer. All the traditional ways of acting and thinking seem to become questionable, yet nobody can imagine how the new world will look. The changes and the uncertainties seem to be greater even than those that followed the breakdown of the medieval world. Now, as then, people are afraid, and do not dare to face the fact that an old world is disappearing and a new one is emerging. They become panicky, and in their panic they stick all the more closely to outmoded political thoughts and methods, seeming to prefer to perish rather than to face uncertainty in an imaginative and courageous manner. They frantically want to preserve the status quo in order to retain some sense of stability, and in the meantime they allay their anxiety by ever-increasing material consumption.

Considering these facts, many people with a sense of responsibility are asking themselves: "Is there anything which might have an effect, and which has not yet been done or tried?" In order to arrive at an answer, one must analyze the reasons for the failure so far. It seems to lie in the following directions:

(1) People's statements have been directed to various aspects of the present crisis; they were not sufficiently global and comprehensive.

(2) They were usually critical and accusatory rather than relying on the power of reason and making an appeal to the human heart.

(3) They were not sufficiently detailed, especially with regard to concrete suggestions about procedures that might lead to a disengagement.

(4) Those who signed the criticisms lacked the authority to be heard and answered by those in power.

The step being proposed in this memo tries to avoid these shortcomings. It is suggested that Pope Paul VI convoke a world conference in Rome to deal with the present crisis of mankind and the possible solutions for engaging it. More specifically, it is suggested that the Pope invite leading personalities of all religions, and also those outside of any religion, of all nations and political creeds, who, because of their achievements and personal integrity, can command the respect of the entire world, to meet in a conference that should last at least four weeks, possibly longer. The purpose of this conference should be to discuss the present critical situation, its causes, and the possible remedies. The conference should arrive at very concrete and specific suggestions for action and procedures toward solving the conflict in Vietnam; furthermore, it should make suggestions for the solution of other urgent problems, as far as possible. These suggestions should be forwarded to all governments through the good services of the Pope, and made public for the information of men in all countries.

It is hoped that such a congress, first of all through the fact that it is convoked by the Pope, and further through the quality and number of its participants, would arouse intense interest over the entire world, and that its deliberations and suggestions would have an intellectual and moral weight that no declaration so far has had. It must also be realized that there is no other personality in the world today, above partisan opinion, whose authority and prestige can compare with that of the Pope. We realize that Pope John and Pope Paul have spoken in unmistakable terms about the need for peace, and they have addressed themselves to all nations in a spirit above all partisanship. Nevertheless, while these declarations made a deep impression on the world, they had only a limited effect precisely because they were necessarily somewhat general in nature and did not confront the various leaders with specific and concrete solutions or suggestions.

It is also realized that the proposal made here suggests a method so far never attempted by the Church, and it could be said that a failure would carry with it the risk of a diplomatic defeat for the Pope. But against these considerations it must be remembered that never before in history has the human race been threatened by extinction as it is now, and that the Roman Catholic Church, as a universal supranational and supraracial organization, has a right—and perhaps the obligation—to take a daring step as long as there is still time.

Such a conference, of course, would need thorough preparation regarding the people to be invited, the proposed agenda, and so on. However, considering the ever-increasing danger, these preparations should be undertaken with the greatest intensity and in the shortest possible time. One might begin by the Pope's inviting a small committee to help in planning the conference. This preparatory committee, like the people who would be invited to the conference, should be chosen without regard for nationality and political or religious affiliation.

To sum up, what seems to recommend this idea is what is new in it: (1) that the conference would be sponsored by the authority and spiritual prestige of the Pope, without being a "religious" conference; (2) that due to this circumstance it is possible to win the cooperation of the widest range of world leaders; and (3) that the conference would go beyond general statements; it would work in a businesslike way and make concrete and specific proposals that would be communicated to the various governments through the good services of the Pope and then be made known to all men on earth.

Finally, it is suggested that it might be helpful if the Pope were approached by a number of leading Catholic and non-Catholic personalities, who would ask him to take the lead in this crusade for peace.

· 8 ·

Campaign for Eugene McCarthy

The following election speech, like the text "The Search for a Human-istic Alternative" in Part I of this volume, is one of Erich Fromm's so-called "memos," an outline for a lecture that Erich Fromm wrote for Eugene McCarthy and that McCarthy gave—with some changes—on June 13, 1968, before the "Fellowship of Reconcili-ation" of the United States in New York. (Founded in England in 1914, the Fellowship of Reconciliation is comprised, according to its charter, of "women and men who recognize the essential unity of humanity and who have banded together in order to explore the power of love and of the truth for the solution of human conflicts.")

The following text is, therefore, an example of Fromm's function as a "ghostwriter" for McCarthy and reproduces Fromm's rough draft. The changes that McCarthy made in Fromm's pre-formu-lated text may be seen at the Erich Fromm Archives, since Eugene McCarthy's modified version is also preserved.

The Fellowship of Reconciliation is an appropriate place to renew my political campaign after the tragic death of Senator Robert Kennedy, who for millions of Americans stood for peace and reconciliation, as did his murdered brother and Dr. Martin Luther King. We need reconciliation in many ways.

First of all, within the country we need the reconciliation of all those who are not sick with hate and despair, whatever their political ideas and concepts are.

We need reconciliation between black and white, based not on vague promises but on real and massive changes in the realm of housing, schooling, and job opportunities.

We need reconciliation between the young and the old generations: The gap between the young generation and its elders has reached the point where mutual understanding has often ceased to exist. My campaign has shown, by its widespread appeal to men and women of all ages, that this reconciliation is possible.

We need reconciliation between our nation and the rest of the world, with those nations which are equal to us in power but also those which are inferior to us in terms of technology and numbers but not in terms of human values and cultural accomplishments. They may learn from us in some respects, but we can also learn from them in many other respects.

We need reconciliation within ourselves—between the values that we profess and the values that motivate us in our daily life. We profess the values and norms of the Judaeo-Christian religion: reverence for life, physically and spiritually; love and compassion, even for the stranger and the enemy; reason and objectivity; the sense of brotherhood of all human beings; and the faith that man is an open system capable of growing to yet-unknown heights.

What are the motivations that move so many of us in our daily lives? Greed, selfishness, hunger for material things, and an indifference to life—which allows us to conduct a war against a small nation, destroying human beings day after day, because we have made it part of our political creed that we must save the freedom of these people, even if we destroy them in the process.

This deep contradiction between ideals and effective values has severe consequences for the nation and for each individual.

For the nation, because it undermines the values that have given our nation vitality and strength; it perverts our leadership in the world from one based on ideals to one based on force. For the individual, because such a deep-seated conflict of values saps his energy and makes him feel guilty. How have we arrived at this impasse?

In the last century it seemed that the machine would be a means to the end of a fuller and richer life, a life that would permit man to develop those faculties and powers peculiar only to him: creative thought, love, and art. Man hoped that, freed from the burden of spending almost all his energy on "making a living," he could build a society in which he was free to be himself, a fully developed man. But man became drunk on his new capacity for what seemed unlimited technological progress. The machine, instead of serving the ends of man, became his master. "Things are in the saddle and ride mankind," as Emerson put it, sensing what was going to happen before it had already happened.

In this process of making material production and consumption the center of human activity, we profoundly changed our value system. We accepted the principle that one *ought* to do what is technically *possible* to do. If it is possible to travel to the moon, we ought to do so, even though at the expense of many unfilled needs on earth; if it is possible to build ever more destructive weapons, we ought to do so, even if they threaten to destroy us and the whole human race. Technical progress threatens to become the source of values, and thus does away with the norm that man has believed in for thousands of years: that one ought to do what is true, beautiful, and conducive to the unfolding of man's soul.

We have accepted another norm dictated by the ever more complex technological system: that maximal efficiency is the highest principle in material production as well as in social organization. The consequence of this principle is the principle of minimal individuality. The more one can cut down a man to easily manageable and predictable units, the more effectively can he be handled. Figures and computer cards demand elimination of fine but important individual differences.

What has become of man in this process?

Man, totally concerned with the production, sale, and consumption of things, becomes more and more like a "thing" himself. He becomes a total consumer engaged in the passive taking in of everything, from cigarettes and liquor, to television, movies, and even lectures and books. He feels lonely and anxious, because he does not see a real meaning to his life beyond that of making a living. He is bored and overcomes his boredom by more and ever-changing consumption and the thrills of meaningless excitement. His thinking is split from emotions, truth from passion, and his mind from his heart. Ideas do not appeal to him because he thinks in terms of calculations and probabilities rather than in terms of convictions and commitments.

Perhaps the greatest danger in our present system lies in the fact that things—gadgets and technical accomplishments—become more attractive than life and growth. Too many of us would like to see ourselves as a "naked ape," combined with a computer brain. If this goal could be accomplished, they think, they have nothing to worry about: Their feelings would remain on the level of the animal activated by instincts and drives, and their thinking would achieve the precision of a computer.

But man is neither an animal nor a computer. If he has no joy and meaningful interest in life, if he senses that his soul is dead while he is physically alive, he becomes bored and begins to hate life and wishes to destroy it. The destroyer is the true opposite of God. It is the nature of God to create; in destroying, man undoes the miracle of creation by an act that requires no skill or talent except possession of a weapon.

It is quite natural that Americans in these days are concerned with the wave of violence, of which the assassinations of political leaders are the most outstanding symptoms. These deeds are only the peek of an iceberg, the bulk of which is an indifference to life and a potential for violence and destructiveness. But it would be a fatal mistake to believe that the cure for violence lies in stricter punishment of crime and greater emphasis on law and order. Irrational violence born of boredom and hopelessness is not cured or diminished by punishments. If life ceases to be attractive and interesting, man becomes desperate and unwilling to renounce the satisfaction of destruction, even for the sake of saving his own life. Indeed, not only increased violence but also increased counterviolence seriously threaten the existence of our democratic system. We must be on our guard that those who do not believe in the democratic process try to strangle it in the name of protecting it.

I submit that the trend of destructiveness and violence can be stopped only when we begin to deal with its real causes rather than with its symptoms. This demands the creation of a new mood in our nation: a mood of hope and love of life, rather than one of hopelessness and attraction merely to the mechanical and lifeless.

Am I preaching an ideal without basis in the minds of the American people? The answer to this question is the most important reason for our hope. While there are many who are resigned to the role of automatons, millions of Americans and, I believe, the majority are aware—explicitly or dimly—of the danger of dehumanization and protest against the further growth of the lifeless consumer society of which I spoke. They are unwilling to surrender their sense of individuality, their values, their hope, their quest for meaningful life, and they insist on a life that responds to their human needs and aspirations. They feel that more care and more gadgets will not make them happy. They appreciate the help that the machine and its products can give to the lives of everybody and do not want to do away with machines nor with computers; but they do not want these to be our masters, for whom we sacrifice our truly human growth. They feel that what matters is to *be more* rather than to *have more* or to *use more*.

This hunger for life is to be found not only in millions of Americans but also all over Europe, particularly among students. They rebel in the name of life against bureaucratic methods of education; and although one may be critical of some of their methods, one must not lose sight of the fact that the violent acts they have committed were violence against *things* and not violence against *life*. There is a great difference between the two.

This new movement in America, the movement for reconciliation and reconstructions for peace and hope, cuts across all traditional, political, and religious groups. It is a common front that reaches from the conservatives—with the exception of fanatical rightists—to radicals—with the exceptions of those despairing and hopeless ones who believe that American society is dead and cannot be resuscitated. While many have surmised that there is such a new front in America, its existence or its size could not be proven, but my campaign has proved it. It is so successful not because I am a saviour or a hero but because I articulate the aspirations of all those Americans who have not lost faith in the past and in the future of our country.

While all of those in this new movement of Americans keep their own ideas and concepts, they share the belief that concepts and words are less important than the substance of a man's personality, which emanates from him. They believe in what Abbé Pire expressed so beautifully: "What matters is not primarily the difference between believers and non-believers but between those who care and those who don't care."

What can be done to reverse the dangerous trends of which I spoke? This is not the moment to give a blueprint for the future, nor can it be given without a great deal of further thought and study by men in business, politics, creative artists, and scholars in human affairs. What matters at the moment is that we change directions, that we move toward a new goal and do not continue to go in a direction that we know leads toward disaster. Whether we go ten miles or one hundred miles in the first year is important, but not primarily so. Let us not forget that the faster one goes in the wrong direction, the sooner one arrives at disaster, whereas even walking less quickly in the right direction gives hope, vision, and patience.

But even if I cannot offer a blueprint for the future, I can outline some specific goals for a new policy.

(1) First of all, we must end the war in Vietnam under conditions that do justice not only to our honor but also to the honor of our opponents, and most of all to the common wish to live and to build. There is certainly a way to peace that can be found, if our offers are credible and if we stop arrogating to ourselves the function of being a policeman over the whole world.

(2) Second, we must put an end to the menace that threatens every human being in our country as well as in the rest of the world: the menace of thermonuclear war. Much can be done to achieve this end. We must liquidate the Cold War atmosphere and arrive at an understanding with the Soviet Union that allows a considerable reduction of armament in both countries.

(3) We must no longer have our policy interfered with by small and often undemocratic governments which get our support only by their claim to be anti-communist. We must redress the anomalous situation of not recognizing the reality of the Peking government and the seven hundred million Chinese which it represents.

(4) If we stop the war in Vietnam and the Cold War, we have the material means and the energy to turn to constructive tasks at home and abroad. The most obvious task at home is massive economic assistance to that sector of Americans who do not participate in the material well-being of the majority. This means new housing facilities in the ghettoes—but not only in the ghettoes, also in those areas outside of cities, in which industry is located and jobs are available. In addition, we must

raise the educational facilities in the ghetto areas in such a way that their inhabitants are capacitated to get the jobs that our technological society offers.

(5) We must, together with other highly developed nations, participate in the task of the economic development of the poor countries. This is best done through agencies of the United Nations. Conditions for such help are that poor nations not be used anymore as pawns in the Cold War and that the best minds of the world be mobilized to work out global programs for this kind of assistance. This may require sacrifices in money. But most Americans will be glad to make sacrifices for purposes that serve life rather than destruction.

There are important aims which, even if briefly indicated, will be immediately understood by many Americans. We must change the kind of bureaucratic method that is now dominant. This method, whether it is employed in factories, schools, universities, or hospitals, is a method that administers people as if they were things. It deprives the individual of all sense of individual initiative and nourishes the belief that the individual can do nothing if it is not planned and organized by the bureaucrats. We must devise another kind of bureaucratic procedure, one that does not make men into its impotent objects but that permits *them* to control the *bureaucrats* and to make their voices heard. If human ingenuity and creativity are freed from deadening bureaucratic methods, new energies will flow into work and productive leisure.

We must not retrench democracy but enlarge it. The individual must have a chance to be a real and responsible participant in all affairs in which he is involved, and must cease to be manipulated by mass suggestion and subtle forms of hypnosis. Experiments with decentralization and with face-to-face groups which are the equivalent of the old town meetings can be most helpful in this direction. We find beginnings already in some advanced methods of industrial management and in many spontaneous group activities all over the country.

America stands today at the crossroads: It can go in the direction of continued war and violence, and further bureaucratization and automatization of man, or it can go in the direction of life, peace, and political and spiritual renewal. There is perhaps no country in which the possibility for such a renewal is as great as in the United States. If we walk the way toward life, America will be able to give leadership and example to the world—not by its might but by its inner strength and imaginativeness. Never has a nation been so clearly confronted with the Biblical saying "I put before you life and death and you choose life!" [Deuteronomy 30:19]. I call on all Americans to help me in giving leadership to the choice for life.

· 9 ·

On the Common Struggle against Idolatry

The dynamics of modern man's alienation and the concomitant question of survival motivated Fromm to the following call for struggle against alienation. The call was directed toward humanistic Christians and bore the title "A Non-Christian Humanist Addresses Himself to Humanist Christians." Composed as a pamphlet in 1975, the call is authenticated by the Centro Intercultural de Documentación (CIDOC), which was founded by Ivan Illich in Cuernavaca, Mexico.

We are witnessing today an historical phenomenon of crucial importance: the almost complete conquest of industrial society by a new paganism. From the beginning of the cultivation of Judaeo-Christian and Greek values and thought until the beginning of the twentieth century, European and North American society had witnessed a rise and flowering of humanism (meaning the supreme concern for the unfolding of those qualities by virtue of which man is man) that did not develop in a straight line, yet constituted a never-interrupted living tradition.

Today we witness the rise of a new form of anti-humanism: of (frequently highly abstract and/or rational) idolatry. This new idolatry does not present itself any longer in the guise of old pagan religions, but as a new paganism that hides quite frequently under the cover of the great Churches and builds what is the essence of anti-Christian, anti-Jewish, anti-Moslem, and anti-Buddhist religiosity.

Idolatry is not the worship of certain gods instead of others, or of one god instead of many. It is a human attitude, that of the reification of all that is alive. It is a man's submission to *things,* his self-negation as a living, open, ego-transcending being. Idols are gods that do not liberate; in worshipping idols, man makes himself a prisoner and renounces liberation. Idols are gods that do not live; in worshipping idols, man himself is deadened.

The modern concept of alienation expresses the same idea as the traditional concept of idolatry. The alienated man bows down to the work of his own hands and to the circumstances of his own doing. Things and circumstances become his masters, they stand above and against him while he loses the experience of himself as the creative bearer of life. He becomes alienated from himself, from his work, and from his fellow man.

Modern man believes that the sacrificing of children to Moloch was a repugnant manifestation of an idolatric past. He would refuse to worship Moloch, or Mars, or Venus and he does not notice that he worships the same idols, only under different names.

Today's idols are the objects of a systematically cultivated greed: for money, power, lust, glory, food, and drink. Man worships the means and ends of this greed: production, consumption, military might, business, the state. The stronger he makes his idols, the poorer he becomes, the emptier he feels. Instead of joy, he seeks thrill; instead of life, he loves a mechanized world of gadgets; instead of growth, he seeks wealth; instead of *being*, he is interested in *having* and *using*.

As a result, modern man has lost any comprehensive system of values except those idolatrous ones; he is anxious, depressed, hopeless, and ready to risk nuclear self-destruction because life has ceased to make sense, to be interesting, and to give joy. If this development is not stopped, nothing will prevent the nuclear catastrophe. Is there still time for change? And whose responsibility is it to work for such change? Whether there is still time left, nobody knows. But can we stop hoping as long as there is still life?

Whose responsibility is it? That of all who are united by their common negation of idolatry. Very specially of all humanists within the Church, representing the oldest Western humanist tradition, speaking with an authority that may touch those who, though idolaters, still have kept a special sensitivity to the voice of the Prophets and the Gospels. Today, it is not the question of converting the heathen to Christianity, it is the question of weaning the Christians and non-Christians away from idolatry. Humanist Christians must speak in their own language about what many thirst to hear: the contradiction between life and things, between ideas and ideologies, between the joy of living and the thrill of consuming. Let it be explained that according to genuine religious tradition the prohibition of idolatry is the condition for all further commandments and concepts. If even ten percent of the population of the Western World could be awakened to a new awareness of the crucial choice, it might mean the difference between catastrophe and life.

How this could be done is a matter for deliberation by those who are concerned and wise. Perhaps an ad hoc committee of men of different religions and from different countries should be organizing this new kind of missionary work. Perhaps one could think of the introduction of a new "ritual" into all meetings held in this context: fifteen minutes of silent meditation. There is only one thing that cannot be compromised: Those who participate must be able to avoid speaking ideologies, they must be able to talk from their heart and to the heart. They must not fear to displease anybody, and must consider that reducing hate and arrogance within themselves must be one of their daily efforts.

· 10 ·

Some Beliefs of Man, in Man, for Man

The "most personal" book that Fromm ever wrote is Beyond the Chain of Illusion: My Encounter with Marx and Freud, *published in 1962. The book begins with an autobiographical chapter and concludes with Fromm's much-quoted "Credo," in which he summarizes, in a sort of confession of belief, his view of man and his insights into the progressive or regressive dynamics of human and social processes. The following "humanist's credo," published here for the first time, is Fromm's humanistic confession of belief. It was presumably written in 1965 as an addendum to his book* The Heart of Man: Its Genius for Good and Evil *(1964).*

• I believe that the unity of man as opposed to other living things derives from the fact that man is the conscious life of himself. Man is conscious of himself, of his future, which is death, of his smallness, of his impotence; he is aware of others as others; man is in nature, subject to its laws even if he transcends it with his thought.

• I believe that man is the product of natural evolution that is born from the conflict of being a prisoner and separated from nature, and from the need to find unity and harmony with it.

• I believe that the nature of man is a contradiction rooted in the conditions of human existence that requires a search for solutions, which in their turn create new contradictions and now the need for answers.

• I believe that every answer to these contradictions can really satisfy the condition of helping man to overcome the sense of separation and to achieve a sense of agreement, of unity, and of belonging.

• I believe that in every answer to these contradictions, man has the possibility of choosing only between going forward or going back; these choices, which are translated into specific actions, are means toward the regressing or toward the progressing of the humanity that is in us.

• I believe that the fundamental alternative for man is the choice between "life" and "death"; between creativity and destructive violence; between reality and illusions; between objectivity and intolerance; between brotherhood-independence and dominance-submission.

• I believe that one can attribute to "life" the significance of continuous birth and constant development.

• I believe that one can attribute to "death" the significance of suspension of growth; continuous repetition.

• I believe that man, with the regressive answer, tries to find unity, liberating himself from the unbearable fear of loneliness and uncertainty, distorting that which makes him human and torments him. The regressive orientation develops in three manifestations, separate or together: necrophilia, narcissism, and incestuous symbiosis.

By *necrophilia* is meant love for all that is violence and destruction; the desire to kill; the worship of force; attraction to death, to suicide, to sadism; the desire to transform the organic into the inorganic by means of "order." The necrophile, lacking the necessary qualities to create, in his impotence finds it easy to destroy because for him it serves only one quality: force.

By *narcissism* is meant ceasing to have an authentic interest in the outside world but instead an intense attachment to oneself, to one's own group, clan, religion, nation, race, etc.—with consequent serious distortions of rational judgment. In general, the need for narcissistic satisfaction derives from the necessity to compensate for material and cultural poverty.

By *incestuous symbiosis* is meant the tendency to stay tied to the mother and to her equivalents—blood, family, tribe—to fly from the unbearable weight of responsibility, of freedom, of awareness, and to be protected and loved in a state of certainty-dependence that the individual pays for with the ceasing of his own human development.

• I believe that the man choosing progress can find a new unity through the full development of all his human forces, which are produced in three orientations. These can be presented separately or together: biophilia, love for humanity and nature, and independence and freedom.

• I believe that love is the main key to open the doors to the "growth" of man. Love and union with someone or something outside of oneself, union that allows one to put oneself into relationship with others, to feel one with others, without limiting the sense of integrity and independence. Love is a productive orientation for which it is essential that there be present at the same time: concern, responsibility, and respect for and knowledge of the object of the union.

• I believe that the experience of love is the most human and humanizing act that it is given to man to enjoy and that it, like reason, makes no sense if conceived in a partial way.

• I believe in the need for "liberty from" internal and/or external ties, as a preliminary condition for being able to have "liberty to" create, build, want to know, etc., to be able to become a free, active, responsible individual.

• I believe that *freedom* is the capacity to follow the voice of reason and knowledge, against the voices of irrational passions; that it is the emancipation that renders man free and puts him on the way to using his own rational faculties and to understanding objectively the world and his own part in it.

• I believe that "struggling for freedom" has in general had the sole meaning of struggling against the authority which is imposed, overcoming individual will. Today, "struggling for freedom" should mean freeing ourselves individually and collectively from the "authority" to which we have submitted "willingly"; freeing ourselves from the inner forces that necessitate this subjection because we are incapable of bearing freedom.

• I believe that freedom is not a constant attribute that "we have" or "we don't have"; perhaps there is only one reality: the act of liberating ourselves in the process of using choices. Every step in life that heightens the maturity of man heightens his ability to choose the freeing alternative.

• I believe that "freedom of choice" is not always equal for all men at every moment. The man with an exclusively necrophilic orientation; who is narcissistic; or who is symbiotic-incestuous, can only make a regressive choice. The free man, freed from irrational ties, can no longer make a regressive choice.

• I believe that the problem of freedom of choice exists only for the man with contrasting orientations, and also this freedom is always strongly conditioned by unconscious desires and by placating rationalizations.

• I believe that none can "save" his fellow man by making a choice for him. To help him, he can indicate the possible alternatives, with sincerity and love, without being sentimental and without illusion. The knowledge and awareness of the freeing alternatives can reawaken in an individual all his hidden energies and put him on the path to choosing respect for "life" instead of for "death."

• I believe that *equality* is felt when, completely discovering oneself, one recognizes that one is equal to others and one identifies oneself with them. Every individual bears humanity inside himself; "the human condition" is unique and equal for all men, in spite of the inevitable differences in intelligence, talent, height, color, etc.

• I believe that equality between men must be remembered, especially, to prevent one man's becoming the instrument of another.

• I believe that *brotherhood* is love directed toward one's fellow men. It will remain, however, a word without sense, until all "incestuous" ties that prevent one from being able to judge the "brother" objectively are eradicated.

• I believe that if an individual is not on the path to transcending his society and seeing in what way it furthers or impedes the development of human potential, he cannot enter into intimate contact with his humanity. If the tabus, restrictions, distorted values appear "natural" to him, this is a clear indication that he cannot have a real knowledge of human nature.

• I believe that society, while having a function both stimulating and inhibiting at the same time, has always been in conflict with humanity. Only when the purpose of society is identified with that of humanity will society cease to paralyze man and encourage his dominance.

• I believe that one can and must hope for a sane society that furthers man's capacity to love his fellow men, to work and create, to develop his reason and his objectivity of a sense of himself that is based on the experience of his productive energy.

• I believe that one can and must hope for the collective regaining of a mental health that is characterized by the capacity to love and to create; by the liberation of man from incestuous ties with the clan and the soil; by a sense of identity based on the experience that the individual has of himself as the subject and agent of his powers; by the capacity to affect reality inside and outside of himself and bring about the development of objectivity and reason.

• I believe that inasmuch as this world of ours seems to become mad and dehumanized, an ever greater number of individuals will feel the need to associate and work with men who share their worries.

• I believe that these men of good intention should not only arrive at a human interpretation of the world, but must point the way and work for a possible transformation. An interpretation without wish for change is useless; a change without preliminary interpretation is blind.

• I believe in the possible realization of a world in which man can *be* much, even if he *has* little; a world in which the dominant motivation of existence is not consumption; a world in which "man" is the end, first and last; a world in which man can find the way of giving a purpose to his life as well as the strength to live free and without illusions.

· 11 ·

Remarks on the Relations between Germans and Jews

Fromm's following "Remarks" on the relation between Germans and Jews are among the last manuscripts that he was able to complete after suffering a severe heart attack in 1977 and a temporary weakening of his short-term memory during the course of 1978. The "Remarks" not only document Fromm's lifelong search for the productive aspects of the relation between Germans and Jews, but are also the personal credo of Erich Fromm, the German-born Jewish humanist, for his observations on Marx, Freud, and Einstein, and their attitude toward power are every bit as befitting of Fromm himself.

Hitler's attempt to destroy the Jewish people has so overshadowed the picture of Jewish–German relations that the relationship between Germans and Jews appears to many as having been essentially negative. But one easily forgets that the approximately one hundred years of German–Jewish cultural coliving resulted in extraordinary achievements. (The Jews had lived in Germany of course since the days of the Roman invasion, but in a cultural as well a local ghetto until the end of the eighteenth century.)

Is it not an amazing phenomenon that the most influential geniuses in the field of the understanding of history, of the human mind, and of nature, should have been German Jews, all born in the nineteenth century—Marx, Freud, and Einstein?

Marx discovered the laws that govern history by showing that the productive forces (human, animal, mechanical, electrical energy) determine the mode of production, which in turn determines the total structure of a society and the class relationships within it. He thus discovered the key to the understanding of history by showing that social and political phenomena are the results of underlying material conditions; he penetrated the surface of historical processes and showed the forces beneath directly observable phenomena.

Freud did something similar for the development of Western thought. He attempted to penetrate the surface—conscious thought—and to arrive at the deep roots of feeling and thought within the individual; he demonstrated that the consciousness of man is the result of influences unknown to himself that originate in his instinctive nature and in the experiences of his early childhood.

Einstein revolutionized man's picture of the physical world, but in contrast to the ideas of Marx and Freud, an adequate idea of his theoretical achievements could be given only by an expert. Nevertheless, he, like Marx and Freud, was characterized by an indomitable faith in reason.

The theories the three men constructed were not positivistic deductions from observable data but were rational visions that were "proved" only many years after their conceptions (or with Freud can never be "proved" in the way to the average person scientific statements are "proved").

Marx, Freud, and Einstein were three German Jews. They were three geniuses who have determined the course of human thought for centuries to come. Inasmuch as no genius is a flower growing in the desert, but needs a soil that permits and furthers its growth, we must assume that this extraordinary productivity of the German–Jewish cultural marriage has its roots in a deep affinity between the Jewish and the German cultures. This affinity is more difficult to grasp today, after we have witnessed the ferocity of anti-Jewish feelings in that part of the German population in which Nazism took its hold. Yet the Jews and the Germans must share some essential qualities that make the fruitfulness of their relationship explainable.

I believe that there is such an essential quality but that it is often ignored because, thinking of Germany, we usually think of the powerful German Empire born in roughly the fourth quarter of the nineteenth century, even though its development had already begun around 1850. Until then, both the Germans and the Jews had been for most of their historical lives nations without power. The powerlessness of the Jews is obvious. The powerlessness of the Germans becomes recognizable also if we compare them with countries like Spain, Portugal, France, and England, which for centuries had been politically and economically powerful nations, succeeding each other in the rulership over a great part of the world. Up to 1871 the Germans could be rightly called "the people of poets and thinkers" (*"das Volk der Dichter und Denker"),* and perhaps nobody represents this anti-nationalistic and anti-militaristic spirit better than one of the greatest Germans living in the period: Goethe, who expressed his scorn for war and nationalism—and very specifically for the so-called War of Liberation—more strongly than anyone else.

I suggest that this *lack of power* is the basis for the deep affinity between the German and the Jewish spirits, and hence a condition for the extraordinary results of their co-living. But it could explain, too, the intensity of Nazi anti-Semitism.

The principle of Nazism was that of expanding the power of Germany. If we consider that the Jewish spirit represented the humanistic and "anti-power" standpoint specific to their own nation's, as well as to that of the earlier German culture, the Nazis were not entirely wrong, from their standpoint, in considering the Jews a danger for Germany. In fact, the Jews were always a danger, and not only for Germany, because *they proved that a people could survive through two thousand years without having any power.* Thus they discredited, if not invalidated, the general belief that power and force—and the two always go together—that seemed to the Nazis to be necessary conditions for national survival.

(When I speak of the Jews I speak of those generations before the present. The power of Hitler and the trauma of the Holocaust have so deeply affected later Jews that most of them surrendered spiritually and believed they had found an answer to their existence in founding a state—which, however, lacks none of the evils inherent more or less in all states, precisely because they are based on powers.)

It would be hypocritical to deny that power was also the governing principle of all major nations. Indeed, to single out Nazism for its bellicosity and striving for conquest is only a subtle device to create the illusion that other powerful nations had acted differently. I am speaking here of course of the principles of Nazi foreign policy, not of their brutal dictatorship within the country.

An obvious objection must be considered here. Were the Jews not quite powerful as bankers and traders in the nineteenth century? Could they not influence foreign policy in the nineteenth century by making loans to various governments? Indeed, through their wealth they did have a political influence although they never had any direct political power. The rich Jews in the nineteenth century remained to a large extent what they had been throughout the Middle Ages—"court Jews" *("Hofjuden")*—which is demonstrated by the undignified flattery and submissiveness of even the richest Jews to kings and the entire feudal class in that century.[1] In fact, when the well-

---

1. See as a good example the relationship between Baron Gerson von Bleichröder and Otto von Bismarck as illustrated by F. Stern in *Gold and Iron*, 1977.

to-do Jews worked for "emancipation" they threw away the pride and dignity that characterized them as long as they were poor. This, of course, is not an exclusively Jewish phenomenon. Pride and dignity, which are characteristics of most societies, necessarily disappear in the bourgeois class in which man is transformed into a commodity. Commodities have a price, but they do not have pride.

The hypothesis presented here must meet with an objection if it is misunderstood to mean that powerlessness and poverty as such are a basis for cultural productivity. Very poor countries can as little afford the luxury of producing geniuses as very "luxurious" countries, and it is obvious that the most powerless countries have not produced the greatest number of geniuses. The optimal conditions seem to be both the absence of great poverty as well as of great wealth.

The German–Jewish cultural intermarriage could bear fruit as long as both cultures had no power. But this was to change in the later part of the nineteenth century. The economic rise of Germany transformed a powerless Germany into the greatest economic and, eventually, military power on the European continent. The German Jews participated fully in the increasing wealth and power of Germany, and by and large lost their traditional condemnation of power. Yet it would be naive to believe that exactly by the year of 1871 the early affinity, based on powerlessness, was completely destroyed.

While Marx (born in 1818) was clearly rooted in the pre-imperialistic period of German history, Freud (born in 1856) was from Austria, which with Hungary formed a weak and unimpressive monarchy that could hardly stir up feelings of admiration concerning the power of his country. (Politically, Germany and the Austro-Hungarian monarchy were of course two separate states. But culturally, Austria and Germany constituted a unity, even though there were some significant nuances between the Austrian-German and the German-German cultures. Albert Einstein (born in 1879) detested power and powerful states, German or otherwise. He was a socialist, internationalist, and pacifist, and he expressed his views very clearly in his writings. When World War I broke out, he was one of the exceedingly few German scholars who refused to sign a patriotic manifesto.

But one fact remains: For the first hundred years of their co-living, the Germans and the Jews had no power and did not glorify power. I believe it was this common ground that brought forth the three German-Jewish geniuses: Marx, Freud, and Einstein.

· PART III ·

Meister Eckhart and Karl Marx on Having and Being

*When Erich Fromm finally moved to Locarno, Switzerland, after
completing his book* The Anatomy of Human Destructiveness
*(1973), he wanted to write a book about Meister Eckhart and Karl
Marx. What bound both thinkers from such different historical and
spiritual contexts was their humanistic concern. Both were concerned
with man and his "salvation of soul." This common interest is contained in the formula "having or being. Fromm became engrossed
in the treatises and German sermons of Meister Eckhart, which,
edited and commented upon by Josef Quint, had been available in
German for a few years. Thirteen years after the publication of*
Marx's Concept of Man *(1961), Fromm again became occupied
with Marx's early writings, and attempted to show the relevance of
Marx's alternative for contemporary man. From this arose sections
of a book about Meister Eckhart and Karl Marx, which he never
published, as well as a manuscript that discussed the relevance of the
choice "having or being" for man in today's society. In view of the
abundance of the resultant material, Fromm wrote in a letter of
December 24, 1974: "I have decided to put the manuscript in two
volumes, one easier and more popular one, which I expect to have
finished in two or three months, and one much more difficult and
theoretical one on the role of religion, its development, and on Marxist socialism as a secular though spiritual phenomenon. The discussion
of the relationship between Eckhart and Marx will remain for the
second volume and only be touched briefly in the first one."*

*In fact, Fromm himself published only the first volume, giving it
the title* To Have Or to Be? *(1976). Most of the manuscript for
the projected second volume follows, published for the first time. From*

113

these hitherto unpublished manuscripts on Meister Eckhart and Marx, Fromm took just several passages pertaining to the interpretation of the "sermon on poverty" and a paragraph or two on the choice "Karl Marx on Having or Being" for To Have Or to Be? *Although these few sections from the original manuscript for the second book have already been published in* To Have Or to Be?, *they are included here for the sake of completeness.*

With the present publication of the manuscript "Meister Eckhart and Karl Marx on Having or Being," all manuscripts written in conjunction with To Have Or to Be? *have been made public. The other posthumously published manuscripts on the topic "Having Or Being" are:* The Art of Being *(New York: Continuum, 1992) and the text "Is Man Lazy by Nature?" (E. Fromm,* Die Pathologie der Normalität, *1991).*

Introduction

The understanding of "having" and of "being" as two different forms of existence will be enhanced if here I give a brief picture of the views that Meister Eckhart and Marx developed on this subject. Not that they are the only ones who have dealt with it; but few thinkers have expressed themselves on the subject with such clarity, depth, and beauty as they did.

Many readers may be surprised to find that these two thinkers can be brought together so closely. Could there be a greater difference than between the medieval Catholic mystic and the "atheist materialist" of the nineteenth century? Indeed, as far as labels are concerned, the difference is unbridgeable. But for a deeper understanding of Eckhart and Marx, one which penetrates to the core of their thinking and makes allowances for the time-conditioned character of their concepts and terminology, the differences are far smaller than what they have in common.

Both were radically anti-authoritarian, spokesmen for the independence of man, for his active use of his essential powers, for life against death, for being against having. For both, reason was the supreme faculty of man. As far as their seemingly diametrically opposed religious views are concerned, Eckhart was an atheist (although thinly disguised); Marx's socialism was the secular expression of prophetic messianism.

Among the socialist authors who have recognized the implicitly religious character of Marx's writings, Ernst Bloch must be mentioned in the first place; I, too, have emphasized the same view.[1] Karl Löwith must be mentioned, and particularly a number of Catholic writers who have understood Marx's writings much better than most "Marxists." Among these are Jean Yves Calvez.

It is also worth mentioning that Eckhart's ideas were highly esteemed by Hegel and some Hegelians. Hegel himself, when Franz von Baader directed his attention to Eckhart, exclaimed (according to von Baader): "Here we have what we wanted!" Also, Hegel's disciples and thinkers closest to his ideas—such as K. Rosenkranz, Johann Eduard Erdmann, and Hans Lassen Marthensen—have carried on this enthusiastic praise of Meister Eckhart.

---

1. E. Fromm, *Marx's Concept of Man,* New York: Continuum (A Frederick Ungar Book), 1961, pp. 58–59 and "Some Post-Marxian and Post-Freudian Thoughts on Religion and Religiousness" (in *Concilium: Internationale Zeitschrift,* vol. 8 [1972], pp. 139–45).

· 12 ·

Meister Eckhart

On the Understanding of His Ideas

Meister Eckhart (1260–1327/29) was the greatest representative of German mysticism and its deepest and most radical thinker. Actively engaged in life as one of the most important figures of the Dominican Order in Germany, he was also a scholarly theologian. But his greatest influence radiated from his German sermons, not only upon his contemporaries and disciples but increasingly again today upon many of those who seek authentic guidance to a non-theistic, yet "religious," philosophy of life.

Eckhart lived at the time of the transition from the high to the late Middle Ages. By the fourteenth century, feudal culture had increasingly given way to the culture of the cities and of the burghers. The dominant "realism"—for which the true being of a thing belonged only to the *idea* contained in it—was losing ground to "nominalism," renewed by William of Ockham (c. 1285–1347), according to which universal concepts were pure *nomina* (names), to which no real beings or things corresponded. True being was to be found only in *individual things,* to be gained only by *empirical observation* and not by abstract-logical speculations. Eckhart himself was, however, an adherent of realism and thus, as F. Mauthner (1920) has pointed out, was able to base his pantheism on the concept of God as the one and all-embracing reality.

As Joseph Quint in the Introduction to Meister Eckhart's *Deutsche Predigten und Traktate* has pointed out, German fourteenth-century mysticism was the result of the fact that the new kind of thinking in that century tended to weaken the intensity of religious experience. I would like to qualify his statement by saying that it weakened the kind of religious experience that was based on philosophical arguments. Thinking did not seem to be the way, anymore, to find God, after thinking itself became subject to critical analysis. In this situation it was almost necessary that a new kind of religiosity should emerge that was different from the metaphysical, philosophical speculations of scholastic thinking, and that would postulate a direct and not intellectually mediated access to God.

At the end of the Middle Ages, faith in God as a vital experience began to vanish because critical thought began to undermine the rational basis for the faith. Today, six hundred years later, the process that began then has almost been completed. Christianity either has become the worship of race, state, power, victory, or charismatic leaders—or it has been frankly abandoned. Eckhart foresaw the development: "Man should not be satisfied with a *thought* God; for if the thought disappears God disappears too," as Quint cites him. Here, for the first time, we hear faintly from Eckhart the motif of a godless, non-theistic religiosity. It was to become louder in Spinoza, and sounded in full strength in the radical humanism of Marx.

Eckhart was the outstanding representative of this new kind of "non-theology." He is called a mystic and rightly so, because his goal is the *unio mystica,* the union of God and man—although, as he says in some of his boldest statements, there is a "something" in man that is *identical* with God and hence does not need to be unified. But he was radically different from many other "mystics" because he abhorred any kind of sentimental, sweet, erotic mood that is enjoyed and wallowed in. This mystic who insisted that one cannot know God by thoughts about him, following the "negative theology" that Maimonides had initiated, removed theological speculation from religious experience, which is "still" and "thought-less." This anti-intellectual had a brilliant and steely intellect, an uncompromising belief in reason. He was gifted with an extraordinary creative language, and was of such a boldness in ideas and expression, that one hardly dares to breathe when he speaks about ideas— of which he tells his listeners that they will probably not understand him.

Eckhart spoke on many levels; usually his views conform with traditional scholastic thinking. On a second level, he was still within the tradition, even though he disagreed with Thomas Aquinas. This level is that of "negative theology," which was first formulated by the Hellenist Jewish philosopher Philo (born 13 B.C.) and found its most elaborate form in the thoughts of Moses Maimonides (1135–1204). Basically, negative theology claims that it is impossible to make any positive statement about God's attributes; this is to say, one cannot say that God is wise, is good, etc. The only statement one can make is a negative one: What God is *not*. The more one knows about what God is not, the greater one's knowledge of God is. The biblical prohibition to giving God a name—except the paradoxical one: I am in the process of being; in other words, "My name is nameless"—contains already the nucleus of negative theology.

But negative theology does in no way deny the being of God; it only denies our capacity to know *what* he is, but not our faith *that* he is. No doubt, negative theology, as Thomas Aquinas had correctly seen, was dangerous to the concept of the Trinity. Yet Eckhart quotes Maimonides more frequently than he quotes any other author, and never with objections.[2] On the other hand, Eckhart did not question the Trinitarian God, except on the level of his non-theism.

---

2. Cf. E. Bloch, *Atheism in Christianity*, New York: Seabury Press, 1970.

On a third level, Eckhart, by implication, denies the being of the Christian God. He does that only in rare statements and in the form of minimizing the significance of the Trinitarian God of Creation in favor of what he calls the "Godhead."

Because of the inconsistency of Eckhart's explicit theological statements, there is great controversy among Eckhart interpreters. In the history of Eckhart interpretation two views oppose each other. One school of thought interprets Eckhart's position as expressing the idea that "God is nothing" and the other as expressing the idea that "God is being." The former interpretation, which puts Eckhart outside Christianity, has been expressed first by Schopenhauer, who in his *Die Welt als Wille und Vorstellung* writes: "Buddha says: 'My pupils reject the idea: this is me, or this is mine.' If one discards the formulations that are due to external circumstances, and goes to the roots of the matter, one will find that Shakia Muni (the Buddha) and Master Eckhart teach the same; except that the former could express his thoughts openly while the latter was forced to clothe them in the garment of Christian mysticism and to adapt his conceptualizations to it."

Other interpreters, too, such as A. Lasson, M. Grabmann, and D. T. Suzuki, represent the "God is nothing" interpretation; Suzuki (1957) has strongly reaffirmed the identity of Eckhart and Buddhist views. Two other Japanese scholars, Minoru Nambara (1960) and Shizuteru Ueda (1965), have analyzed the "God is nothing" aspects of Eckhart and thrown more light on his affinity with Buddhism, and G. Stephanson's 1954 analysis is very helpful for the understanding of Eckhart's concept of the Godhead.

In the most recent decades, the majority of interpreters of Eckhart have interpreted him as a Christian theologian of God's being, and have regarded the statements by Eckhart that indicate the opposite either as purely allegorical or as needing to be interpreted in the light of his dominant orthodox theological views. These interpreters have made use of a seemingly compelling argument: Not only are Eckhart's non-theistic statements in rare contrast to his orthodox statements, they are also not to be found in those writings that are declared by J. Quint as being of proven authenticity. However, this argument is, after some further analysis, not as compelling as it seems at first glance.

In the first place, as Quint states, his inclusion of various parts of Eckhart's writings in the *Deutsche Werke* is provisional "and does not decide the authenticity or non-authenticity of other *non*-included texts of sermons and tractates in the Pfeiffer and other editions. Unquestionably there is among this material further genuine Eckhart texts."[3]

Second, we can speak of Eckhart the person and writer, but we can also speak of "Eckhart" as a collective name for the writings of Eckhart and of his school. It does not make really a great deal of difference whether the boldest expression of the theology of Nothing was only developed by his immediate students. The difference would be that one could not speak of contradictions within Eckhart that could be resolved by depth analysis.

But there is no need to fall back on this concept of the Eckhart school, because even in the writings that are declared as proven to be authentic, we find clear expressions of Eckhart's most radical views; and those who have neglected this "radical" Eckhart and supported their position by the "authenticity" argument, have simply neglected to consider these authentic statements.

As already stated, Eckhart arrives at a non-theistic view through the concept of the Godhead. The Godhead is "untouched" by Man, his ideas, his imagination, and his concepts. In another not (yet) authenticated statement,[4] Eckhart speaks in reference to the verse "God is a true light that shines in the

---

3. J. Quint, *Deutsche Predigten und Traktate*, Munich, 1969, p. 537.
4. Cited by F. Pfeiffer, *Meister Eckhart*, Göttingen, 1924.

darkness, of three kinds of darkness" (John 1:9), saying: "The third darkness is the very best, and means that there is no light, it is neither cold nor warm in itself." While these above statements are not judged to be of proven authenticity, the following is judged, by J. Quint, to be authentic: "What is the final goal? It is the hidden dark of the eternal Godhead and is unknown and was never known, and will never be known. God is there unknown to himself and the light of the eternal father has eternally shone into it, but the darkness does not comprehend the light (John 1:5)."[5]

In his Sermon *Beati pauperes spiritu,* Eckhart says: "My essential being is above God [the Trinitarian God]. In that being of God, where God is above all Being and all distinctions, there I was myself, there I wanted myself and knew myself willing to create this man (myself). That is why 1 am the cause of myself in my Being, which is eternal, not in my becoming, which is temporal. And that is why I am unborn and according to my unbornness I can never die, have been eternal, and am now and shall be forever.... In my eternal birth all things were born and I was the cause of myself and of all things; and if I had wanted, neither I nor things would exist; but if I did not exist, 'God' [the Trinitarian God] would not exist either; I am the cause that God is God; if I were not, God would not be 'God.' To know this is not necessary.

"A great authority says: 'His bursting forth is nobler than his efflux.' When I flowed forth from God, creatures said, 'He is a god!' This, however, did not make me blessed, for it indicates that I, too, am a creature. In bursting forth, however, when I shall be free within God's will and free, therefore, of the will of God, and all his works, and even of God himself, then I shall rise above all creature kind, and I shall be neither god nor creature, but I shall be what I was once, now, and forevermore. I shall thus receive an impulse that shall raise me

---

5. Quint, op. cit., p. 261.

above the angels. With the impulse, I receive wealth so great that I could never again be satisfied with a god [the God of the Bible] or anything that is God's, nor with any divine activities, for in bursting forth I discover that God [the Godhead] and I are One. . . .

"If anyone does not understand this discourse, let him not worry about that, for if he does not find this truth in himself, he cannot understand what I have said—for it is a discovered truth that comes immediately from the heart of God. That we all may so live as to experience it eternally, may God help us! Amen."[6]

While the foregoing statements and another (Sermon 15 in Blakney; see below and Bibliography) do not yet speak directly of the Nothing, the following authenticated sentence does; and it proves that Eckhart has personally—not only his school—expressed the idea of God as Nothing: "And if God is neither goodness, nor truth, nor ONE, what then is he? *He is nothing, he is neither this nor that.*" This from the sermon *Jesus hieß seine Jünger aufsteigen.*[7]

Eckhart never explicitly denies the existence of the Trinitarian God. But he reduces his importance by pointing out that "God" and the "Godhead" are as far apart as heaven and earth. The Godhead is absolute and "mysterious" darkness, unknown to himself; absolutely passive, resting in himself, the Nothing; he himself is identical with the *"Seelengrund,"* the ground of Man's soul, which is also the absolute Nothing.

This view is not any longer Christian or theistic, but it is Eckhart's "secret" view, which came to his consciousness only a few times in sermons, when he seemed to have been inspired and in a semi-trancelike state. Only if one deals with Eckhart's writings as a closed system without immanent contradictions can one come to the conclusion that Eckhart's non-theistic

---

6. R. B. Blakney, *Meister Eckhart: A Modern Translation,* New York, 1941; some re-translation by E. Fromm.

7. S. Ueda, *Die Gottesgeburtinder Seele . . .* Gütersloh, 1965.

statements can be ignored. If one understands Eckhart's writings as the utterances of a creative man, full of contradictions, and on rare occasions expressing his usually "repressed" thoughts can one understand his role as one of the earliest representatives of non-theistic "religiosity." On the level of non-theism Eckhart shares with Buddhism—and as we shall see, with Marx—the position of radical metaphysical skepticism.

Metaphysically speaking, the last reality for Eckhart is death, the Nothing. Life is not given any meaning by an absolute—not even the Christian God. The answer to this objective meaninglessness of life is human activity, in caring for the well-being of our fellow creatures. Shizuteru Ueda has summarized this point very succinctly: "The radicalism and the peculiarity of Eckhart's view of the *vita activa* and *vita contemplativa* lies in the fact that for him both are not ways *toward* God, but ways away from God. The way to God is, for him, as we saw, not *vita* but only death, complete detachment. The *vita activa* for Eckhart means away from God to the reality of the world, together with breaking through God (the God of Creation) to the Godhead. Activity in this sense occurs without God; a deed like bringing soup to a sick person is nothing but this work itself; it is without added religious meaning."

On Having and Being

A condition for understanding Eckhart's concept of having–being is being aware that Eckhart deals with the underlying motivation, whether it be conscious or not, and not with overt behavior. Quint justly calls him an "extraordinary analyst of the soul" saying: "Eckhart never tires of uncovering the most secret ties of human behavior, the most hidden stirring of selfishness, of intentions and "opinions," of denouncing the passionate longing for gratitude and rewards."[8]

---

8. Quint, op. cit., p. 29.

This insight into the hidden motives makes Eckhart so appealing to the post-Freudian reader, who has overcome the naiveté of pre-Freudian and still-current behavioristic views which claim that behavior and opinion are two final data that can be as little broken down as the atom was supposed to be at the beginning of this century. Eckhart expressed these views in numerous statements, of which the following is characteristic: "People should not consider so much what they are to do as what they *are*. . . . Thus, take care that your emphasis is laid on *being* good and not on the number or kind of things to be done. Emphasize rather the fundamentals on which your work rests." The *being* of a person is the reality, the "spirit that moves him," the character that impels his behavior, in contrast to the deeds or opinions which, separated from the dynamic core of the person, have no reality.

Eckhart shows an extraordinary capacity for discovering the unconscious egoism behind behavior which, consciously, is conceived as its very opposite. He shows how behind the good works, the prayers, the fasting, a great possessiveness is hidden. "You degrade the infinite God to a milk cow, which one esteems because of her milk and cheese, because of the profit she brings," he says. Or: "They make a goat of God, feed him with leaves of words. Or they make an actor of God and give him their old, miserable clothes." When they are lucky, says Eckhart in his Sermon 48, "they praise God and trust in him, as some say: 'I have plenty of corn and wine this year, I fully trust in God.' Quite right, I say, you have full confidence—in the corn and the wine." And: "You bargain with your God, you give and work, so that he returns your gift a thousandfold; this giving should be rather called a craving," Eckhart admonishes.

To have nothing means to make oneself "empty," to free oneself from all ego-bound strivings, to overcome one's self-centeredness. Quint describes Eckhart's thought very succinctly: "The works of the just man are always *alive,* because their rank is solely determined by the great noble attitude, and its impulses are not rooted in the *dead* layer of the ego-bound, temporal Konrad or Heinrich but in the alive innermost nucleus of the essential man, one with God."[9] I quote Quint's statement here particularly because he emphasizes an element in Eckhart's thought that is of particular importance in the context of this study; I refer to juxtaposition of the *deadness* of the ego-bound possessive orientation, in contradistinction to the *aliveness* of the non-possessive core of man.

Can Eckhart's radical concept of God only be understood in the context of his critique of the "property structure of existence"? "No," says Eckhart, "the temple (i.e., man) must be free and unfettered, as the eye must be free and empty of all colors, if it is to perceive color. But all those images and imaginations are a beam in your eyes. Hence, throw them out of your soul, all Saints and Our Lady, because they are all creatures and are an obstacle to your great God."

Eckhart, by differentiating between God and Godhead, made it possible to make statements that were not necessarily as drastic as if he had only *one* concept of God, yet they were bold enough and constituted an important part of his alleged heresy. Eckhart's "God" is the traditional God of the Bible, who created the world and is active. His Godhead did not create the world, he is completely inactive; he is the "silent desert," the unmoved *and unmoving*—the Nothing. Eckhart speaks of "God" when he asks the Godhead, "Please get me rid of God," in the sermon *Beati pauperes spiritu*. As Quint summarizes Eckhart's view: "You should rid yourself even of your "thought" God, of all your inadequate thoughts and imaginations about him, such as: God is good, is wise, is just, is infinite, God is not good, I am better than God; God is not wise; I am wiser than He. To call God a being is as senseless as it would be to call the sun pallid or black. If I had a God whom I could grasp, I would never recognize Him as my God. Hence, be silent

---

9. Ibid., p. 40.

and don't bark about Him, don't hang on Him the clothes of attributes and qualities, but take Him without quality, as He is "a being above being" and "a nothingness transcending being in the still desert of the nameless Godhead."

This is essentially Maimonides' negative theology, but it led to its same ultimate consequence, having no concern where the thought might lead—or how it might be misunderstood. Eckhart does not make dogmatic, final, well-balanced statements here. He shouts passionately saying, in effect: As long as you hold on to anything, even to God, you will never be free and you will never experience God in yourself.

Eckhart denounces the property structure of existence as the evil that stands in the way of man's freedom, his aliveness, his finding himself. But there could be no greater misunderstanding than to think that Eckhart's ideal was a passive, or even a completely contemplative, life. A quick glance at his life shows that this cannot have been so. He was the head of the Dominican Order in Saxony, the general vicar of the Dominican Order in Bohemia, a teacher at the University of Paris, the head of the Dominican convent in Strasbourg; and finally, he was called to the chair at the Studium Generale in Cologne, where Albertus Magnus had taught. He was a man of action, a leader of men, how could he have recommended extreme isolation and passivity? Indeed, he did not.

For Eckhart the abandonment of having, clinging, craving, the giving up of the mode of having, the inner "expropriation," as Mieth calls it, meant creating the condition for the fullest activity—not of *trivial* but of *essential* activity. Productive, "essential" activity, he believed, was possible only under the conditions of freedom, and we were free only if we did not cling to what we had—including our ego. Eckhart said something, more generally and more radically, that many people know: Giving excludes holding on; loving requires one to drop one's ego. One who is preoccupied with himself cannot love; even sexual functioning requires concentration.

The problem, according to Eckhart's teaching, is *not that I have nothing, but that I am not egocentrically bound to what I have*. This is the decisive point in Eckhart's teaching about poverty and not having. While traditional thinking offered the alternative between having much (luxury) and having nothing (ascetic poverty), Eckhart cut through this alternative and showed its illusionary character: The man indulging in luxury and the ascetic depriving himself of everything both share the egocentric mode of having—the one by affirmation, the other by negation. The real opposition is that between the ego-bound man, whose existence is structured by the principle of having, and the free man, who has overcome his egocentricity, "who eats when he wants to eat and sleeps when he wants to sleep." (This Eckhart's statement is almost literally the same as the Zen statement that the enlightened person "sleeps when he sleeps and eats when he eats.")

For the free man, all he has is merely an instrument for greater aliveness; it does not matter whether he has more or less, because he is himself! Everybody is able to have the same experience. If he can attain a state of mind in which he is not preoccupied with anything, still, concentrated, not holding on to anything, he will experience unusual strength and vitality if he turns to something he feels like doing. Out of this stillness he acquires the energy for action—but only for essential action (i.e., action that corresponds to his essence as man). He needs has irrational stimulations from the outside, if he has to be motivated by irrational passions. This movement can be expressed in many ways; "only through losing myself do I save myself;" "if I have nothing, I am everything;" "the greatest poverty is the greatest wealth." (The same difference is to be found in Buddhist teaching. The Buddha was against asceticism. He taught that *craving* causes suffering, but that there is also a detached, nongreedy having, which can be enjoyed without causing suffering. (The latter principle is more emphasized in Mahayana than in Hinajana Buddhism.)

The Sermon on Poverty

The classic source for Eckhart's views on the mode of having is his sermon on poverty, based on the text of Matthew 5:13: "Blessed are the poor in spirit, for theirs is the kingdom of heaven." In this sermon Eckhart discusses the question *What is spiritual poverty?* He begins by saying that he does not speak of external poverty, of a poverty of things, although that kind of poverty is good and commendable. He wants to speak of inner poverty, the poverty referred to in the gospel verse, which he defines by saying: "He is a poor man who *wants* nothing, *knows* nothing, and *has* nothing."

(1) Who is the person who *wants* nothing? A man or woman who has chosen an ascetic life would be our common response. But this is not Eckhart's meaning, and he scolds those who understand not wanting anything as an exercise of repentance and an external religious practice. He sees the subscribers to those concepts as those of people who hold on to their selfish egos. "These people have the name of being saintly on the basis of the external appearances, but inside they are asses, because they don't grasp the true meaning of divine truth."

For Eckhart is concerned with the kind of "wanting" that is also fundamental in Buddhist thought; that is, greed, craving for things and for one's own ego. The Buddha considers this wanting to be the cause of human suffering, not enjoyment. When Eckhart goes on to speak of having no "will," he does not mean that one should be weak. The will he speaks of is identical with craving, a will that one is *driven* by—which is, in a true sense, *not* will. Eckhart goes so far as to postulate that one should not even want to do God's will, since this, too, is a form of craving. *The person who wants nothing is the person who is not greedy for anything*—this is the essence of Eckhart's concept of non-attachment.

(2) Who is the person who *knows* nothing? Does Eckhart establish that it is one who is an ignorant, dumb being, an

uneducated, uncultured creature? How could he, when his main effort was to educate the uneducated and when he himself was a man of great erudition and knowledge that he never attempted to hide or minimize?

Eckhart's concept of *not knowing anything* is concerned with the difference between *having knowledge* and the *act of knowing,* the latter implying penetrating to the roots and, hence, to the causes of a thing. Eckhart distinguishes very clearly between a particular *thought* and the *process* of thinking. Stressing that it is better to know God than to love God, he writes: "Love has to do with desire and purpose, whereas knowledge is no particular thought, but rather it peels off all [coverings] and is disinterested and runs naked to God, until it touches him and grasps him."[10]

But on another level (and Eckhart speaks throughout on several levels) Eckhart goes much further. He writes: "Again, he is poor who knows nothing. We have sometimes said that man ought to live as if he did not live, neither for self, nor for the truth, nor for God. But to that point, we shall say something else and go further. The man who is to achieve this poverty shall live as a man who does not even know that he lives, neither for himself, nor for the truth, nor for God. More: He shall be quit and empty of all knowledge, so that no knowledge of God exists in him; for when a man's existence is of God's external species, there is no other life in him: his life is himself. Therefore, we say that a man ought to be empty of his own knowledge, as he was when he did not exist, and let God achieve what he will and man be unfettered."

To understand Eckhart's position, it is necessary to grasp the true meaning of these words. When he says that "a man ought to be empty of his own knowledge," he does not mean that he should forget *what* he knows, but rather he should forget *that* he knows. This is to say that we should not look at our knowledge

---

10. An Eckhart statement cited by Blakney but not authenticated by Quint.

as a possession, in which we find security and which gives us a sense of identity; we should not be "filled" with our knowledge, or hang onto it, or crave it. Knowledge should not assume the quality of a dogma, which enslaves us. All this belongs to the mode of having. In the mode of being, knowledge is nothing but the penetrating activity of thought—without ever becoming an invitation to stand still in order to find certainty.

(3) Eckhart continues: What does it mean that a man should *have* nothing? "Now pay earnest attention to this: I have often said, and great authorities agree, that, to be a proper abode for God and fit for God to act in, a man should also be free from all [his own] things and [his own] actions, both inwardly and outwardly. Now we shall say something else: If it is the case that a man is emptied of things—creatures, himself, and God—and if still God could find a place in him to act, then we say: As long as that [place] exists, this man is not poor with the most intimate poverty. For God does not intend that man shall have a place reserved for God to work in, since true poverty of spirit requires that man shall be emptied of God and all his works, so that if God wants to act in the soul, He himself must be the place in which He acts. . . . Thus we say that a man should be so poor that he is not and has not a place for God to act in. To reserve a place would be to maintain distinctions. *Therefore, I pray God that He may quit me of god.*"

Eckhart could not have expressed his concept of not having more radically. First of all, we should be free from our own things and our own actions. This does not mean that we should neither possess anything nor do anything; it means we should not be bound, tied, chained to what we own and what we have, not even to God.

For Eckhart, independence is a necessary condition of being; his concept of independence is a very radical one, as can be seen from the following sentences: "Whoever accepts something from another is a servant; and whoever rewards, a master. I was wondering the other day whether I should accept something from God, or wish something from Him. I shall ponder about it quite seriously because if I would accept [something] from God, I would be under God like a servant and He, by giving, like a master. But this should not be so in eternal life." Or, in terms of human equality: "I say, manhood in the wretchedest most despicable man is as perfect as in king or pope. . . ."

The following paragraph is Quint's summary of Eckhart's position: "But what is the attitude of the 'God-owned,' great man toward life? It would seem as if this empty vessel, which wants nothing, has nothing, and knows nothing, [and] in spiritual poverty, is only good to gaze dully and inactively in the still desert of the infinite. But no, this is what put on Eckhart's mysticism the unmistakable stamp of Occidental world feeling, the stamp of infinite lust to become and to act, so that, for Eckhart, eternal quiet in the Lord is only thinkable and imaginable as eternal driving and becoming. The still desert of God's infinite rational being is, for the vital thinking of Eckhart, comparable to an infinite fiery flow of metal, which, boiling continuously, penetrates itself with itself before it flows out into created being."

We have arrived here at Eckhart's concept of the negation of having: the condition *"of freeing the essential man for essential activity in a world released to essential being, so that man can become an active and loving member of his group."*

· 13 ·

Karl Marx

The *"Religious"* Interests of Marx

If the discussion of Meister Eckhart's concept causes difficulties for those who either cannot reconcile his implicit atheism with his explicit theology, and also for those for whom the use of the word "God" is a shibboleth that makes them reject the author as an "authoritarian" and "reactionary," the difficulty with the understanding of Marx's ideas is even greater. Soviet communism has been so successful in distorting and corrupting Marx's ideas (and incidentally convincing the West that "Soviet Marxism" was the true interpretation of Marx) that it is very difficult to rid oneself of this distorted picture.

The difficulty in understanding Marx lies in the fact that Soviet Marxism and reformist Western socialists alike present Marxism as essentially and exclusively concerned with economics. They have interpreted "historical (or dialectic) materialism"—terms that Marx himself did not use—to mean that the main driving force in man is his passion to have and consume more and more and have proclaimed that socialism was meant to be a better means to achieve greater production and consumption for all. Only a relatively small number of Marxist scholars—among them pro- and anti-Marxists—have pointed out that Marx's final goal was not *economic* but *human* change; and that the idea of the primacy of the drive for possession is a bourgeois and not a Marxist concept. Marx assumed the greed for money to be the *product* of certain social circumstances, not an "instinct" that was the *cause* of these circumstances. His aim was the liberation of man from crippledness, from his loss of himself, from his alienation. The socialist society was not an aim in itself, but a means to the full realization of man.

Marx's was in the deepest sense a non-theistic religious system, concerned with the salvation of man, a reformulation in secular language of the ideals of prophetic messianism.

Excursus: Religion and the Concept of God

Any attempt to demonstrate the religious nature of Marx's system meets with almost insurmountable obstacles. The first obstacle, of course, lies in the term "religious," which is generally understood to imply the belief in God. This is a typically European-centered provincialism. Confucianism, Taoism, and Buddhism were religions, yet they had had no concept of God. The European [or Western] religions—Judaism, Christianity, and Islam—used the symbol of God, because Near Eastern social and political organization suggested symbolizing the supreme value by the concept of a supreme father or king. Europeans were arrogant enough through the centuries to proclaim the white man's symbol to be constitutive for any religion. While this was the popular feeling, the theologians solved the problem more elegantly by speaking of "primitive" forms of religion, in which the lack of full development had not led to the recognition of God as a supreme being. As a result, almost everybody reacted to the word "religious" as he would react to the concept of God. One could bypass this difficulty by using the phrase "spiritual" instead of "religious," and I shall do so sometimes. (And needless to say, the word "spiritual" has associations to "spiritualism," which also tend to vitiate it.)

The difficulty in finding a proper word for an atheistic religiosity lies of course not in the scarcity of right words but in the historical fact of the development of European thought. Christian belief, as formulated by the scholastics and given its final systematization by Thomas Aquinas, had a concept of God that tried to reconcile its two different sources: the Biblical God of immediate experience and the Aristotelian "philosophical God" of thought, the "unmoved mover." The existence of the Biblical God of experience could be "proven" by philosophic argument, in line with Aristotle. At a period in which no alternative explanation for the miracle of Creation could be offered, when the existing geocentric picture of the universe was virtually unquestioned, there was no problem in this identification of the two Gods. On the contrary, what worthier witness for the teaching of the Bible could be found than the greatest of all philosophers, Aristotle? However, by the very greatness of his achievements, the reconciliation between faith and reason, Thomas Aquinas (1225–74) opened up a development that eventually should prove to be dangerous, if not fatal, for religion. With the change of philosophical thought from an abstract and unempirical approach (by this I do not imply that one can ignore the empirical scientific aspects of Aristotle's philosophy) to concrete, critical, and eventually scientific thinking, the philosophical foundation of religion became shaky.

Thomas Aquinas, like other scholastics, had taught that one could prove the existence of God by philosophical argument. What became of this proof when the progress of critical and scientific thought, together with new discoveries, offered alternative explanations to the miracle of Creation and the "lawfulness" of nature? From Galileo to Darwin, the myth of the special place of man among the creatures, rooted in the belief in the Biblical traditions, was more and more undermined; science offered alternative and more convincing explanations. Since the scholastic had anchored religion in a thought concept—the provable belief in God—what would become of religious experience when the thought concept lost its validity?

The fourteenth century opened up a new mode of thinking that led directly to the concrete, critical mode of thought which was to become the basis of scientific thought—and of technical development. (Lewis Mumford has justifiedly warned against the current cliché that the Middle Ages were "static," and that there was no technical progress before the Renaissance.) The problem is that of the acceleration of invention brought about by the new form of thinking and other important social factors. The decisive figure in the new philosophical development was [England's] William of Ockham (c. 1285–1349), the most outstanding philosopher of the fourteenth century.

Ockham's significance, both as a theologian and as a philosopher lay in his rejection of the metaphysical assumptions of medieval realism, which taught that an intelligible order of abstract essences and necessary relations was ontologically prior to, that is to say, more "real" than, particular things and contingent events, and hence that the intellect can demonstrate first causes and eventually the existence of God. Ockham, in a radical opposition to this view, reconstructed philosophy on the basis of radical empiricism, in which the evidential basis of all knowledge is direct experience of individual things and particular events. Ockham's faith in God could neither be refuted nor proven by philosophical reasoning or observational evidence.

By Ockham's radical departure from scholastic metaphysics, his theological emphasis shifted from *thinking about* God, to the immediate and subjective experience. Furthermore, he freed faith in God from the danger that scientific insights could destroy it. The intellect could neither prove nor disprove the existence of God; only inner experience could be the basis of faith. The opinions that the thought concept "God-as-supreme-ruler" was itself historically conditioned, and that if it were not for the Near Eastern origin of Christianity this particular concept would not have been chosen, were of course alien to the thought climate of the fourteenth century. When the emphasis shifted from the thought concept to the experience, the former lost its significance.

This development was brought to its final point by Eckhart. As we have seen, Eckhart's radical formulation of "negative theology" led to a non-theology. The God of Creation—the active god—lost his supreme role, and the "Godhead," far above the God of Creation, was no god to think about, to talk about, or even to talk to. He was stillness and silence, he was no-thing. What alone mattered was man, the process of inner liberation, his efforts to become a just being. Eckhart, of course, used the traditional symbol, but he gave it a new content.

It is not without interest to speculate what would have happened if Eckhart's non-theology had become representative of Christianity, instead of Thomas Aquinas' beliefs. In such a hypothetical (and, for historical reasons, impossible) case, religion would have been as little affected by scientific progress as, for instance, Buddhism could be. Then, religion would not have been challenged by militant atheism, which is the logical consequence of a God-centered religion; instead, critique would have challenged religion immanently, by demonstrating that it failed to contribute to man's development according to its own premises. (This immanent criticism was Marx's and not a position of "atheism" in the conventional sense.) Eckhart shifted the emphasis from theology to anthropology.

Spinoza's (1632–77) was another attempt to shift the center of religion from God to man, from theology to ethics. He, too, continued to use the concept God, but by equating God with nature he denied the traditional concept of God even more radically and openly than Eckhart could have done three centuries earlier. Spinoza was concerned with the norms that lead to man's optimal development. His idea was to realize that margin of freedom that is man's in spite of the fact that man's life was determined by circumstances outside his control. The way: ceasing to be a slave of irrational passions and developing only affects that grow in the soil of inner freedom—generosity and fortitude, all-embracing love and strong courage.

In contrast to Eckhart, Spinoza was no theologian in the sense that he practiced a particular religion and represented its theology. He did not express his ideas in the vernacular but in Latin, and thus only reached primarily other philosophers. For this reason he could not have influenced religious development directly. But the influence of his ideas on the thinking of the next two centuries was tremendous, as is indicated by the fact that Goethe, Hegel, and Marx were deeply influenced by Spinoza (Marx excerpted in great detail Spinoza's writings, as his notebooks indicate).

However, neither Eckhart nor Spinoza had a great influence on the development of *religious* thought as such. Eckhart lived too early for that, so that papal authority could brand him as a heretic; Spinoza, also branded by the Jewish community in Amsterdam as a heretic, had no home in any religion.

Official Christianity did not make the shift from the emphasis on the God concept to the emphasis on human experience. And thus it was bound to lose more and more adherents, who could not integrate the philosophical concept of God with the new scientific mode of thinking and the great discoveries resulting therefrom. However, it was not simply that the new thinking destroyed faith in God. Even today, a majority of the inhabitants of Western Europe and North America may state that they believe in God, but this belief has lost all relevance for their personal lives. It does not motivate the believers to live a "religious life"; God is a rather pallid symbol, socially shared and satisfying some residual needs as a "helping Father," especially when life is dangerous. In fact, this philosophical God has become an idol, unified with the idols of secular authority.

I need hardly add the qualifying remark that there are exceptions to this rule. And we see these exceptions even growing in the last decades: Albert Schweitzer, Pope John XXIII, Archbishop Dom Helder Camara and the hundreds of Catholic priests, especially in Latin America, for whom religion is not centered around theology (i.e., the *right thoughts about God*) but around the demand for an active life of love, justice, and responsibility for each other. But they are still the minority.

The mainstream of historical development has led to this alternative: Religion = belief in the traditional God concept or in the secular life given to egoism, greed, and violence. Dostoevski once formulated this alternative quite succinctly: "If God is dead, everything is permitted." He meant that if I do not believe in the symbol God anymore, I cannot lead a life based on the norms and values that were implied in a faith in God; it appears that the door to salvation is closed to all who, for any number of reasons, cannot state, "I believe in God." However, since the council convened by Pope John XXIII, there are many theologians who do not say this, and who see the way to salvation open also to those who do not believe in God. (The arguments for this position differ from Karl Rahner's that one can never know whether somebody who says that he believes or does not believe in God may deceive himself, and that conscious disbelief may cover factual belief and vice versa. The arguments would be compatible with Eckhart's position that the thought belief is irrelevant, by comparison with whether a person acts as a believer would—or should—according to his faith.)

The crucial question today seems to me to be the following: Was Dostoevski right with his alternative? Or is there a "religious" attitude, or way of life, that is legitimate and authentic, although it does not include the concept of God? Is our culture destined to arrive at the point where *man* is dead—after God is dead? Are we to resign to the life of greed and possessiveness, and thus to lose our soul, because we cannot extricate ourselves from a King-God concept that stamped our conceptual thinking about 3,000 years ago? Is there a future for a new "atheism," one that is deeply religious and opposed to the theistic idolatry that is dominant?

Undoubtedly there is a yearning for a new kind of "atheistic religiosity." One can observe it among the young in many Western countries. It became manifest in such phenomena as the "hippies," the interest in Yogi, Zen Buddhism, and similar phenomena. But a good deal of it fell by the wayside or was exploited by individuals and groups interested in publicity. The most profound ideas—from the Delphic "Know Thyself" to Freud's analysis—were prostituted; from fake gurus to equally fake prophets of joy and sex, nothing remained uncontaminated by the poison of contemporary publicity-seeking and commercialism.

As a result, resignation reigns among many, who now return to the old gods because the new ones have proved to be false. Obviously, however, this method of becoming enlightened in quick lessons—by drugs, weekend instructions, attempts at false intimacy and whatnot—had to fail, for nothing serious is accomplished without great effort, patience, and honesty. But there is no reason to be disappointed when one discovers that false ways cannot lead to desired goals.

Karl Marx followed the paths of Eckhart and Spinoza; the goal of his atheistic *radical humanism* was the salvation of man, his self-actualization, the overcoming of the craving for having and consumption, his freedom and independence, and his love for others.

Humanism as Secular Messianism

The most important overall statement to be made is that Marx's radical humanism was a system aiming at the salvation of man, a principle that it had in common with Buddhism and Judaism and Christianity. "Salvation" is, of course, a term that has been monopolized by the European religions and hence seems to imply a reference to God, who is or who sends a Savior. Buddhist salvation has no such connotation. It teaches that man has to save himself; he is only supported in this task by the wisdom of the Buddha, who is a teacher, not a savior.

To keep the concept of salvation free from its theistic coloring, it is helpful to remember its literal meaning. Salvation, like the French *salut* and the Spanish *salud,* comes from Latin *salvare,* the root of which is *sal,* or salt. Salt was used to keep meat from decomposition; literally speaking, salt "saved" the meat. Applied to man, then, salvation means that he is saved from decomposition and in thus being saved he is healthy *(salut).* By whom and from what man is saved is another matter. Buddhism said from suffering, inherent in all greed; Christianity has taught that he is saved from "original sin"; Judaism, that he is saved from the consequences of living wrongly and, specifically of idolatry; and Marx taught that man is to be saved from alienation, from the loss of himself.

In this point Marx's philosophy differs essentially from the mainstream of Greek thinking, N. Lobkovicz,[1] a very learned opponent of Marx's system, has pointed to this fundamental difference very succinctly: "Aristotle philosophizes out of 'wonders,' out of an intellectual curiosity that is half awe, half the desire to adjust man's existence to the order of being, the cosmos. Both Hegel and Marx, on the contrary, philosophize out of unhappiness and dissatisfaction, out of the 'experience' that the world is not as it ought to be. Accordingly, while Aristotle primarily aims at understanding, at discovering structures and laws to which man's thought and actions have to adjust, Hegel and Marx aim at 'reconciling' and/or revolutionizing.

"In Aristotle nothing is or even can be wrong as it is, in its natural state. The problem for Aristotle does not consist in correcting the universe or in making it rational; it consists in discovering its inherent order and rationality and in adjusting oneself to it. In Hegel and Marx almost everything is wrong

---

1. In N. Lobkovicz, *Theory and Practice: History of a Concept from Aristotle to Marx,* Notre Dame/London, 1967, pp. 340ff.

and consequently has to be transfigured, transformed, revolutionized. In this respect the only truly important difference between Hegel and Marx is that Hegel is still enough committed to the Greek philosophical tradition to believe it possible to reconcile man with the universe by teaching him adequately to understand it, while Marx, disappointed with Hegel's speculative transfiguration, has lost all faith in the healing and reconciling power of mere thought."

One may add to Lobkovicz's description that Marx's concept of salvation is very close to the messianic concept of some of the Old Testament prophets. The "Messianic Time" was to be not a transcending, but a historical period in which all mankind would be united in peace, where aggression and fear would have disappeared, and where the knowledge of God would cover the whole earth.[2] This salvation was not an act brought about by God's grace, but the result of man's own efforts to find the way to his own perfection. To be sure, this version of messianism was not the only one, and in the post-prophetic period was to a large extent overshadowed by another version quite in opposition to the first. This second version was the catastrophic, or apocalyptic. Briefly, the Messiah would come when man had reached the state of the most complete dehumanization, as a result of which destructive wars and catastrophes would have occurred. Only at the height of this catastrophe would the Messiah be sent by God, and not, as in the first version, as the result of man's own achievements. The Jewish Talmud, indeed, states that there is this alternative between the two concepts: that the Messiah will come in an age that is either fully pure or fully corrupt (Sanhedrin 98a).

The fact that the first version by no means disappeared can be seen in many Talmudic utterances and in Maimonides' de-

---

2. Cf. the detailed presentation of Messianism in E. Fromm, 1966, and the opposite position in G. Scholem, 1963. In Micha, not even the common worship of the God of the Hebrews is required, but every nation will pray to its own God.

scription of the messianic time. He states, declining the catastrophic theory: "And in that time there will be no famine and
no war; and no envy and no strife. The goods of the world will
exist in abundance; and all comforts will be as plentiful as dust.
The whole world will only be concerned with knowing God.
Hence, Israelites will be very wise and know things that are
now concealed, and will arrive at a knowledge of their creator,
as far as the mind is capable of, as it is written (Is. 11:9): 'For
the earth will be full of the knowledge of the Lord, as the
waters cover the sea.' "[3]

I differ in this interpretation from that given by G. Scholem
(1963). Scholem, in line with his general position that the concept of the messianic age was to be virtually a catastrophic
one, comments on the above-quoted statement by Maimonides:
"Their [Maimonides' words] soberness codifies the protest
against apocalyptical thinking, against the fertile fantasy of the
Haggadists, against the authors of the popular Midrashim, in
which the various steps to the end and the catastrophes of
nature and history are described that accompany it. This all is
wiped out with a marvelous gesture. Maimonides knows nothing of messianic miracles and other signs. The messianic time
brings about negatively 'the freedom' from the present servi-
tude of Israel and, as a positive content, the freedom for the
knowledge of God; but for this purpose neither the law of
the ethical order, the revolution of the Torah, or the law of the
natural order need to be changed."

Scholem in these remarks seems entirely to ignore the fact
that an order in which there is no envy and no war, and plenitude of things for all people, is by no means sufficiently described as "freedom" for Israel from slavery and "freedom for
the knowledge of God." It is indeed a utopia, but not the *apocalyptical* utopia of the change of the law of nature and of the
existence of man; it is the *historical* utopia, that of an entirely

---

3. Moses Maimonides, *Mishne Torah. Book of Judges*, Chap. 12; my translation.

new form of living which includes all man. Even though it is true that Maimonides has made a number of statements about the messianic time that do not contain this radical vision, he has made it and, in fact, it constitutes the last sentence of his magnum opus, *The Codification of the Law.*

The elements in Marx's concepts of socialism are all here: absence of envy, of aggression, of war and the plenitude of all things for all. The only difference is that for Maimonides this means the knowledge of God, while for Marx it refers to man's full grasp of the world through reason and love. (The last great Jewish philosopher, the Neo-Kantian Hermann Cohen, has very explicitly made the connection between messianism and socialism.)

The difficulty in understanding Marx's system lies in the fact that it is generally assumed that Marx was a representative of "progress," as it was conceived in the liberal-bourgeois sector of industrial society. This concept of progress consisted in maximal knowledge (education), maximal industrial production, maximal consumption. As Carl L. Becker (1946) showed so succinctly, the future—"posterity"—had assumed the role of the heavenly kingdom; man sought for immortality, or at least for the justification of his existence, by participating in building the future, i.e., progress in the above-mentioned sense. The striving for immortality is expressed in modern man in his craving for fame or notoriety (to be known by others is an affirmation of one's existence), for being of historical importance (the latter especially among the political leaders), or for being at least a witness of historical events. Progress was infinite in time, since there could never be an end to the increase of production and consumption; perfection in infinite time had taken the place of inner perfection in life-time.

Marx was as opposed to this concept of progress as conservative thinkers such as Disraeli were. The conservatives, like Marx, saw that the continuation of the pan-economism of the industrial system would lead to the slow destruction of the human substance, and create a soulless, helpless man. In this respect their views are sometimes extremely close to Marx's. The main difference was that they believed they could stem the evil by saving the old economic structure (and thus serving the interests of the class that they represented), whereas Marx, not being a Romantic, believed that the threat to man could only be overcome by a complete new social structure, which was neither that of feudalism nor of capitalist industrialism, but of socialism—in which all men would be able to enjoy things without becoming their slaves. Marx's opposition to the liberal-industrial ideas of progress is generally overlooked, because soon socialism began to ally itself with liberalism and to affirm "progress," except one that was extended to the working class as well. As a consequence of this blindness, one either ignored or did not take seriously enough the truly revolutionary character of Marx's doctrines. To be sure, Marx wanted a political revolution that would lead to a social revolution (a revolution like the democratically organized Paris Commune was to him a shining example). But what constitutes the truly revolutionary character of Marx's ideas was the *human* revolution, the new phase in human life, a phase that would end prehistory and be the beginning of *human* history.

Marx's thinking was related to that of J. G. Fichte and that of, indeed, Schiller. For Fichte (1762–1814), as for his contemporary, Schiller, history was the dimension in which man's evolution took place; it was the evolution from an existence governed by instincts to one based on autonomous reason. In the process, these "instincts" were codified and transformed into an "exterior coercive authority," Fichte wrote, in his own time. Eventually man would rebuild himself to a perfect embodiment of reason, and history would culminate in an epoch of "accomplished justification and sanctification." N. Lobkovicz adds that "Fichte's description of the age of 'accomplished sinfulness' anticipates Hegel's (and Marx's) analysis of 'civil society.' Abandoned by his instincts and still not having reached knowledge *(Wissenschaft)*, man is reduced to 'mere naked individuality' and the species—'the only thing that truly exists'—degenerates into an empty abstraction. With reason *qua* instinct having withered away and autonomous self-conscious reason still not being within man's reach, 'there remains nothing but mere individual, personal life.' No wonder, then, that the 'present age' knows only one virtue, 'shrewdness *(Klugheit)*, in pursuing one's personal advantage.' "[4]

Schiller's ideas on the subject were in many ways similar, and the same scheme is to be found in Hegel too. In the ideas of Fichte, Schiller, Hegel, then, the central topic is man and his self-evolution, not by grace but by his own effort. The same holds true for Marx's concepts. He praised Hegel's *Phänomenologie des Geistes* because Hegel had shown here that the emergence of man's humanity was a "process of human self-procreation," the story of man's coming to be! What is new in Marx is that he discovered economy as the misery that blocked man's way to his self-realization, and that not only the growth of man's reason but of all his intellectual, emotional, and sensory faculties was the goal of his becoming human.

But Fichte and Schiller offered primarily a philosophy of history. Hegel still believed that the philosophical understanding of history was enough to bring about the great change. Marx blended philosophical insight with revolutionary faith and action, and challenged all philosophers of the past with the statement "The philosophers have only *interpreted* the world indifferently; what matters is to *change* it."[5]

This famous sentence has usually been understood as the call for political and socio-economic revolution, which it was. Marx, the man intensely involved in politics, could be legitimately interpreted in this way. But, as I noted before, Marx's revolutionary intent was much bolder and, if one likes, more utopian. It was a call to man, not only to *think* differently and

---

4. Ibid., p. 317.
5. K. Marx and F. Engels, MEGA. Part 1, 6 vols. Berlin, 1932, Vol. 5, p. 535.

to *act* differently but to *be* different. The revolution aimed for a new man and a new society—humanly, and not only politically or economically, speaking. Marx joins the revolutionary tradition of messianism that had been first expressed by the prophets, then by the Cabbalists, by Joachim of Floris (1145?–1202), by Eckhart. His goal was not that of liberal ethical reform, nor was it that of the middle-class progressive (including Freud). It was the utopian one of the new world, as it had never existed.

Marx has given various expressions to his messianic vision. Man by his own activity creates himself in history ("History does nothing," says Marx); he becomes fully human when he has reduced the effort to sustain himself by work to a minimum, when he has overcome egotism, when he is unselfishly related to others, when he has attained full independence from any outer power, when he is a wealthy man because he *is* much and not because he *has* much.

Marx gave the new form of individual and social existence the name "communism," but he has never given a concrete description of what communism would be, except in terms referring to man. His concrete political program, as it is expressed in the *Communist Manifesto,* is exceedingly modest, seen from the observation point of the second half of the twentieth century, when most of its demands are fulfilled in a number of capitalist countries. By not outlining in any concrete way what the communist society would be like, Marx kept the purity of his vision without having to compromise it by concrete descriptions that would be obliged to anticipate developments that could not be anticipated in the old society and by the as yet unchanged man. Marx only described what communism was not.

If we read his description of communism, it fits in many ways a "socialist" country like the Soviet Union:

> Communism as universal private property appears in a double form; the domination of material property looms so large that it aims to destroy everything that is incapable of being pos-

sessed by everyone as private property. It wishes to eliminate talent, etc., by *force*. Immediate physical possession seems to it the unique goal of life and existence. The role of *worker* is not abolished, but is extended to all men. The idea of private property remains the idea of the community to the world of things. Finally, this tendency to oppose general private property to private property is expressed in an animal form: *Marriage* (which is incontestably a form of *exclusive private property*) is contrasted with the community of women, in which women become communal and common property. One may say that this idea of the *community of women* is the *open secret* of this entirely crude and unreflective communism. Just as women are to pass from marriage to universal prostitution, so the whole world of wealth (i.e., the objective being of man) is to pass from the relation of exclusive marriage with the private owner to the relation of universal prostitution with the community. This communism, which negates the *personality* of man in every sphere, is only the logical expression of private property, which is this negation. Universal *envy* setting itself up as a power is only a camouflaged form of cupidity which reestablishes itself and satisfies itself in a different way. The thoughts of every individual private property owner are at least directed against any *wealthier* private property, in the form of envy and the desire to reduce everything to a common level; so that this envy and leveling in fact constitute the essence of competition. Crude communism is only the culmination of such envy and leveling-down on the basis of a preconceived minimum. How little this abolition of private property represents a genuine appropriation is shown by the abstract negation of the whole world of culture and civilization, and the regression to the *unnatural* simplicity of the poor and wantful individual who has not only not surpassed private property but has not yet even attained to it.[6]

Marx described this new society as "the real appropriation of the human essence by and for man; the complete return of man to himself as a social, that is, human being—a return to becoming conscious and accomplished within the entire wealth

---

6. Ibid., Vol. 3, pp. 111ff.

of previous development. This communism, as fully developed naturalism, equals humanism and, as fully developed humanism, equals naturalism; it is the genuine resolution of the conflict between man and nature and between man and man—the true resolution of the strife between existence and essence, between objectification and self-affirmation, between the individual and the species. Communism is the riddle of history solved, and it knows itself to be this solution."[7]

At the end of his life's work, in *Das Kapital,* Marx continues the same line of thinking. "Man will have reached that point of history where he can realize his human task: the development of his powers for their own ends. *But it always remains a realm of necessity.* Beyond it begins that development of human power *which is its own end* [my emphasis]: the true realm of freedom, which, however, can flourish only upon that realm of necessity as its basis."

The new era will be that of the ultimate completion of every human being, "the consummated essential oneness of nature and man, the true resurrection of nature, the naturalism of man and the humanism of nature both brought to fulfillment."[8] In the new society man will achieve equality. For Marx, equality refers to the unity of the human essence, the practical identity of man with man, that is, for the social or human relation of man to man.

Having and Being, According to Marx

From the background of Marx's revolutionary humanism, his atheistic messianism, can we now hope to form an adequate understanding of his concept of *having* and *being*? The most important element in Marx's concept of having is the same as that of Eckhart's: the distinction between having something to

7. Ibid., Vol. 3, p. 114.
8. K. Marx and F. Engels, MEGA, Part 1, Vol. 3, p. 116.

be used and enjoyed and the *sense of possession* that is a mode of existence.

In contrast to the corrupted version of Marx, which says that his aim was that the worker should *have* more and eventually as much as the capitalist and thus share in the progress that brings happiness (= unlimited consumption for all), Marx considered the orientation of *having* as the central defect of man in capitalist society. "Private property," he wrote, "has made us so stupid and partial that an object is only ours when we have it, when it exists for us as capital, or when it is directly eaten, drunk, worn, inhabited, etc., in short, *utilized* in some way. . . . Thus *all* the physical and intellectual senses have been replaced by the simple alienation of all these senses via the sense of having. The human being had to be reduced to this absolute poverty in order to be able to give birth to all his inner wealth."[9]

The "sense of having" about which Marx speaks here is precisely the same as the "ego-boundness" of which Eckhart speaks, the craving for things and for one's ego. Marx refers to the *having mode of existence*, not to possession as such, not to unalienated private property as such. The goal is not luxury and wealth, nor is it poverty; in fact, both luxury and poverty are looked upon by Marx as vices.

In the passage quoted above, Marx speaks of poverty, which he equates with the total sense of having. In other words, the man who *has* much is a poor man, and not a rich man as he believes himself to be. But this very poverty is the condition for giving birth to his inner wealth.

What is this act for "giving birth"? It is the active, unalienated expression of man's faculty toward the corresponding objects: "All his [man's] *human* relations to the world—seeing, hearing, smelling, tasting, touching, thinking, observing, feeling, desiring, acting, loving—in short, all the organs of his individuality . . . are in their objective action [their *action in relation to the*

---

9. Ibid., Vol. 3, p. 118.

object] the appropriation of this object, the appropriation of human reality."

This is the form of appropriation in the mode of *being*, not in the mode of *having*. Marx expressed this form of non-alienated activity in the following passage: "Let us assume man to be man, and his relation to the world to be a human one. Then love can only be exchanged for love, trust for trust, etc. If you wish to enjoy art, you must be an artistically cultivated person; if you wish to influence other people, you must be a person who really has a stimulating and encouraging effect upon others. Every one of your relations to man and to nature must be a *specific expression*, corresponding to the object of your will, of your *real, individual* life. If you love without evoking love in return, i.e., if you are not able, by the manifestation of yourself as a loving person, to make yourself a beloved person, then your love is impotent and a misfortune."[10]

For Marx, the wealth of a human being lay in his capacity to express his needs; but these needs in themselves were the product of history and not innate instincts. For an understanding of Marx's concept of needs, the following passage is important:

> The distinctive character of each faculty is precisely its *characteristic essence* and thus also the characteristic mode of its object-ification, of its *objectively real, living being*. It is, therefore, not only in thought, but through *all* the senses that man is affirmed in the objective world.
>
> Let us next consider the subjective aspect. Man's musical sense is only awakened by music. The most beautiful music has no meaning for the non-musical ear, is not an object for it, because my object can only be the confirmation of one of my own faculties. It can only be so for me insofar as my faculty exists for itself as a subjective capacity, because the meaning of an object for me extends only as far as the sense extends (only makes sense for an appropriate sense). For this reason, the *senses* of social man are different from those of non-social man.

10. Ibid., p. 149.

It is only through the objectively deployed wealth of the human being that the wealth of subjective human sensibility—a musical ear, an eye that is sensitive to the beauty of form, in short, senses that are capable of human satisfaction and that can be confirmed as human faculties—is cultivated or created. For it is not only the five senses, but also the so-called spiritual senses—the practical senses: desiring, loving, etc., in brief, human sensibility and the human character of the senses—that can only come into being through the existence of *its* object, through humanized nature. The cultivation of the five senses is the work of all previous history. Sense that is subservient to crude needs has only a restricted meaning. For a starving man the human form of food does not exist, but only its abstract character as food. It could just as well exist in the most crude form, and it is impossible to say in what way this feeding activity would differ from that of animals. The needy man, burdened with cares, has no appreciation of the most beautiful spectacle. The dealer in minerals sees only their commercial value, not their beauty or their particular characteristics; he has no mineralogical sense. Thus, the objectification of the human essence, both theoretically and practically, is necessary in order to *humanize* man's senses, and also to create the *human senses* corresponding to all the wealth of human and natural being.[11]

Marx's critique of the political economists is that "they forget that production of too many *useful* things results in too many *useless* people ... [and] that prodigality and thrift, luxury and abstinence, wealth and poverty are equivalents." Marx's concept of wealth and poverty mean the opposite of what they mean to classic economy and in popular usage: "... in place of the *wealth* or *poverty* of political economy, we have the *wealthy* man and the rich human need. The wealthy man is at the same time one who *needs* a complex of human manifestations of life, and whose own self-realization exists as an inner necessity, a need. Not only the *wealth* but also the *poverty* of man acquires, in a socialist perspective, a human and thus a social meaning. *Poverty is the positive bond that leads man to experience a need for the*

---

11. Ibid., pp. 119ff.

greatest wealth, the other person [emphasis added]. The sway of the objective entity within me, the sensuous outbreak of my life-activity, is the passion that here becomes the *activity* of my being."[12]

Marx did not propose an ascetic ideal, which would imply that abolition of property means not enjoying anything, nor did he believe in the ideal of a maximum of property and consumption for all, which Krushchev once called, approvingly, "goulash-communism." Marx, in contrast, stated that *poverty and luxury were equivalents*. He made his opposition to the idea of ever greater income and consumption for the workers very clear in the following passage:

> An enforced increase in wages (disregarding other difficulties, and especially that such an anomaly could only be maintained by force) would be nothing more than a *better remuneration of slaves*, and would not restore, either to the worker or to the work, their human significance and worth.
> Even the *equality of incomes* that Proudhon demands would only change the relation of the present-day worker to his work into a relation of all men to work. Society would then be conceived as an abstract capitalist.[13]

The central theme of Marx is the transformation of alienated, meaningless labor into productive, free labor, not the better payment of alienated labor by a private or state capitalism.

Contemporary "labor" leaders from [the AFL's George] Meany to [the U.S.S.R.'s Leonid] Brezhnev counter this position by pointing to the worker's needs which are his natural right to have fulfilled; and the capitalist agrees in principle, except that the satisfaction of these needs should be properly geared to his profit rate. Marx, on the other hand, opposes this whole argument concerning human needs. Not only does he distinguish between genuine and artificially produced needs,

12. Ibid., pp. 123ff.
13. Ibid., p. 92.

but also, and more important, he shows that increasing needs enslave and dehumanize man.

The dependence on unessential needs, i.e., on needs that are not rooted in the essential powers of man, was clearly seen by Marx at a time when it was much less obvious than it is today. The following passages in Marx show succinctly how, for Marx, "alienated need," just as alienated property, cripples man and makes him dependent:

> Every man speculates upon creating a new need in another in order to force him to new sacrifices in order to place him in a new dependence, and to entice him into a new kind of pleasure and, thereby, into economic ruin. Everyone tries to establish over others an alien power in order to find there the satisfaction of his own egoistic need. With the mass of objects, therefore, there also increases the realm of alien entities to which man is subjected. Every new product is a new potentiality of mutual deceit and robbery. Man becomes increasingly *poor as a man*; he has increasing need of money in order to take possession of the hostile being. The power of his money diminishes directly with the growth of the quantity of production; i.e., his need increases with the increasing *power* of money. The need for money is therefore the real need created by the modern economy—and the only need that it creates. The *quantity* of money becomes, increasingly, its only important quality. Just as it reduces every entity to its abstraction, so it reduces itself in its own development to a *quantitative* entity. Excess and immoderation become its true standard. This is shown subjectively, partly in the fact that the expansion of production and of needs becomes an *ingenious* and always *calculating* subservience to inhuman, depraved, unnatural—and *imaginary*—appetites. Private property does not know how to change *crude* need into *human* need; its idealism is *fantasy, caprice,* and *fancy*. No eunuch flatters his tyrant more shamefully or seeks by more infamous means to stimulate his jaded appetites in order to gain some favor than does the eunuch of industry, the entrepreneur, in order to acquire a few silver coins or to charm the gold from the purse of his dearly beloved neighbor. Every product is a bait by means of which the individual tries to entice the essence of the other person, his money. Every real

or potential need is a weakness that will draw the bird into the lime. [There is] universal exploitation of the common human essence.[14]

Marx could hardly have spoken more clearly. This passage shows the unbridgeable gap between Marx's concept of progress and that of "capitalists" and Soviet-socialists alike. While they define *progress* as the greatest happiness (read: consumption) for everybody, hence recommending their respective systems as being most conducive to maximal consumption, Marx sees in this progress a great danger: the growth of dependence. The more man's needs grow, the more dependent he grows. Dependent on whom? In the first place, on those who create those needs by their ability to sell the corresponding satisfactions, making others dependent on them. Second, because the more the needs and satisfactions grow, the poorer becomes man as man, and the more he is dependent on the satisfaction of depraved, inhuman, imaginary appetites, until eventually he becomes a self-propelled commodity.

Marx touched, here, on the crucial question we have just begun to debate. The question is whether we ought to strive for increasing production and consumption, i.e., for wealth and luxury, or whether we should restrict production and consumption to human proportions, i.e., to a level where it does not contribute to man's laziness and alienation but furthers his capacity to use his faculties productively. Briefly, whether progress lies in *having* more or in *being* more.

Marx's answer was unequivocal; it was based on his insight into the psychological consequences of the contemporary system of maximum need-creation and need-satisfaction.

Marx has called the spirit of *having*, which permeated the capitalism of his time, a spirit of asceticism:

Political economy, the science of *wealth*, is therefore, at the

---

14. Ibid., pp. 127ff.

same time, the science of renunciation of privation and of saving, which actually succeeds in depriving man of fresh *air* and of physical *activity*. This science of a marvelous industry is at the same time the science of *asceticism*. Its true ideal is the *ascetic* but *usurious* miser and the *ascetic* but *productive* slave. Its moral ideal is the *worker*, who takes a part of his wages to the savings bank. It has even found a servile art to embody this favorite idea, which has been produced in a sentimental manner on the stage. Thus, despite its worldly and pleasure-seeking appearance, it is a truly moral science, the most moral of all sciences. Its principal thesis is the renunciation of life and of human needs. The less you eat, drink, buy books, go to the theater or to balls, or to the public house, and the less you think, love, theorize, sing, paint, fence, etc., the more you will be able to save and the greater will become your treasure, which neither moth nor rust will corrupt—your capital.[15]

What did Marx mean by *being*? The most general attribute of being is "free, conscious activity," which he considered to be "the species character of the human species." The qualifications "free" and "conscious" indicate that Marx used the term differently from its modern usage, in which to be active means "to do something," whatever it may be; as for instance, to use an extreme example, the activity of an obsessional person of walking for hours in his rooms, exactly three paces forward and three paces backward; or, to use an example that is perhaps not less extreme but less obvious: the activity of a bureaucrat to write reports on insignificant events, and another to read the reports, and a third to file them. Marx's concept of activity is close to that of the Aristotelian scholastic tradition. For Aristotle [in his *Ethica Nicomachea*], "human good turns out to be activity of soul in accordance with virtue, and if there are more than one virtue, in accordance with the best and most complete." Hence, of course, contemplation can be the highest form of activity.

15. Ibid., pp. 129ff.

Free and conscious activity means that the person is the author of his activity, i.e., that he is not active by exterior or inner compulsion; *conscious* activity means that the subject knows what he is doing, and is not acted upon by forces behind his back. We know what Marx meant by "species character": the non-egotistical man, related to others and feeling his solidarity with them.

Marx has given further descriptions of this free and conscious activity. His central thesis is that such activity is the active-productive use of man's real—not imagined—faculties and powers (Marx says "essential powers" since they belong to the essence of man). These powers are brought to life and expressed toward objects which or who can be their proper recipients.

What Marx is saying is that man needs an object for the expression of his faculties; that his essential powers are endowed with the dynamic quality of having to strive for an object they can relate to and unite themselves with. *The dynamism of human nature is primarily rooted in this need of man to express his faculties toward the world, rather than in his need to use the world as a means for the satisfaction of his physiological necessities.* What Marx is saying is that because I have eyes I have the need to see; because I have ears I have the need to hear; because I have a brain I have the need to think; and because I have a heart I have the need to feel. In short, because I am a man, I am in need of man and of the world.[16]

In this state of experience, the separation of subject from object disappears; they become unified by the bond of human active relatedness to the object. In this context one must understand—and can only understand—Marx's concept of the "crippled man," "man's return to himself," and "the wealthy man."

In *Das Kapital* [Vol. 1, p. 534], Marx speaks of the "crippled worker," the "mere fragment of a man." This characterization

---

16. Cf. E. Fromm, "Man's Contribution to the Knowledge of Man," in *Social Science Information*, 1968, p. 10.

implies an uncrippled, "non-fragmented" worker who has reestablished his full humanity. In this sense Marx can speak of the final goal (called communism) as being *"the return of man himself as a social, i.e., really human, being* [some emphasis mine], a complete and conscious return that assimilates all the wealth of previous development."

Among the specific manifestations of free, conscious activity, *loving* takes an eminent place, for Marx. In his polemic against Edgar Bauer, who had spoken of love as of a "cruel goddess," Marx argued that Bauer transformed the *loving man*, the *love of man* into a *man of love*—"by separating the 'love' from man and making it a being apart from him, and thus making love into something independent . . . love, which teaches man truly to believe in the world of objects outside of himself, which make not only the [other] man an object for us, but also the [non-human] object into a man!" This idea is very important: Not only are the social bonds constituted by love, but belief in the reality of the world itself, outside of us, is founded on our quality of loving. But, Marx continues, Bauer was not only attacking love as a human activity but, with it, "everything alive, everything immediate, all sensuous experience, all *real* experience in general, of which one never knows "wherefrom" or "whence."[17]

The words "everything alive" are key words in Marx's ideas about being. *Being refers to life* and to the present; *having, to death* and to the past. Behind the allegedly purely economic concepts of capital and labor are anthropological concepts that give the battle between capital and labor its spiritual, passionate character. This is by no means a theoretical speculation. Marx has expressed it very explicitly. In *Das Kapital*, he—and not the young Marx—writes: "Capital is dead labor; that vampire only lives by sucking living labor, and lives the more, the more labor it sucks." In the *Communist Manifesto* he puts the alternative

---

17. K. Marx and F. Engels, MEGA, Vol. 3, pp. 190ff.

between capitalism and communism in the following terms: "In the bourgeois society, therefore, the past dominates the present; in communist society, the present dominates the past. In bourgeois society capital is independent and has individuality, while the living person is dependent and has no individuality."[18]

Life and death, past and present, free activity vs. unfree activity, labor and capital, independence and submission, growth and crippledness are so many different aspects of Marx's fundamental dichotomy—*being* and *having*—which is of course the cornerstone of his whole system. The following sentence is one of the many formulations:

> The less you *are,* the less you express your life, the more you *have,* the greater is your *alienated* life and the greater is the saving of your alienated being. Everything that the economist takes from you in the way of life and humanity he restores to you in the form of *money* and *wealth.* And everything that you are unable to do, your money can do for you; it can eat, drink, go to the ball and to the theater. It can acquire art, learning, historical treasures, political power; and it can travel. It can appropriate all these things for you, can purchase everything; it is the true *opulence.* But although it can do all this, it only desires to create itself, and to buy itself, because everything else is subservient to it. When one owns the master, one also owns the servant, and one has no need of the master's servant. Thus, all passions and activities must be submerged in *avarice.* The worker must have just what is necessary for him to want in order to live, and he must want to live only in order to have this.[19]

---

18. K. Marx, *The Communist Manifesto,* trans. S. T. Possony, Chicago, 1954, p. 44.
19. K. Marx and F. Engels, MEGA, Vol. 3, p. 130.

·14·

The Common "Religious" Concern

The Tradition of Mysticism

When Marx speaks of a "sense of having," he means precisely the same thing that Eckhart called "ego-boundness"; when Marx uses poverty as the condition for being, his terminology is even identical with that of Eckhart.

In other respects, general opinion sees great differences, when they scarcely exist. This holds particularly true for two problems: the role of rationality and of worldly activity. The mystic Eckhart is supposed to be an opponent of rationality and of worldly activity, hence quite obviously irreconcilable with the "rationalist" and activist Marx. This misrepresentation rests upon the popular and almost universal misunderstanding of mysticism in general and Eckhart's mysticism in particular.

Mysticism is more or less identified with "mystification," and it is supposed to suffer from a lack of rational clarity, to dwell in the realm of feeling and pious enchantment, and furthermore to imply flight from the social reality and consist of worldly passivity and a continuous state of mystical contemplation. To be sure, there are mystics for whom this description is more or less correct. But it is completely false as far as Eckhart and certain other mystics, such as the author of *The Cloud of Unknowing* and (Pseudo-) Dionysius Areopagita, is concerned. For the full understanding of Eckhart's mysticism, I ask the reader to follow me in a detour that, inadequate as it is by its sketchiness, should help in the understanding of him.

Classic Judaism and, following its conceptualizations, Christianity and Islam are religions of monotheism. They worship the One God, in contrast to the pagan worship of many gods. This difference between the One and the many is not a quantitative but a qualitative one. The One is the supreme principle of knowledge and of ethics. It has not only emerged in the Near East, but also in India and China, and often in a purer form than in the [Western] concept of the One God.

It seems to me a reasonable hypothesis to assume that at a certain point of human development, when man had cut most of the primary ties that still made him a part of the soil and of his tribe and when individuation had reached its first peak, man had to become more aware of himself as an individual being confronted with the manifoldness of phenomena—those things that were "not I"—which stood in opposition to him. As a consequence, a logical need had to develop; namely, that of distinguishing the phenomenal world, the world of the many, from another principle that stood opposite the phenomenal world, the principle of the One, or the No-thing, in order not to be overwhelmed by the deceptive veil of the manifoldness of things.

Man must have had the same experience with himself, too. At the same first peak of individuation, the laws and norms of his primary group became less effective and he was overwhelmed by the manifoldness of his desires and wishes; the more objects he created, the more desires were awakened; he would become a helpless bundle of desires unless he could build the idea of the One in himself, experience himself as the subject of desires and actions, formulate a concept of self or of I.

Thus the search for the principle of the One as a regulating principle of cognition and self-experience became a necessity—unless man was to become the helpless object of things and of his senses. It should be noted that the process of individuation occurs in several steps. The first step is the emergence of men from the animal kingdom (described in my *Anatomy of Human Destructiveness,* 1973, and earlier works referred to in this book). The second step occurs at a certain point, in Near Eastern civilization, from the Neolithic Age (9000 B.C.) to the highly developed civilizations of the first and second millennia B.C.; and the next step is at the turn from medieval to industrial culture, which I have described in my book *Escape from Freedom* (1941).

In India the principle of the One was established in the earliest parts of *The Upanishads.* It is called the Brahman, the principle of the One in the universe, which is identical with the Atman, the principle of the One in the person. This One is not somebody or something; it transcends all being, having no other name than that it is not something. It is the supreme principle of world, often also defined as *neti, neti* (i.e., "It is not this and is not that"). (But side by side we find also in *The Upanishads'* conceptualization of the Brahman as Supreme Father, something hardly distinguishable from Old Testament language.)

In Mahayana Buddhism the highest truth is absolute voidness (emptiness), which can be hinted at only by what is *not.* Thus we find in Indian thought the beginning of negative theology.

In Chinese thinking we find the same idea expressed in Taoism. The *Tao Te Ching* begins with this sentence: "The Tao about which something can be said is not the absolute Tao. The names that can be given are not the absolute names. The Nameless is the origin of heaven and earth" (my translation).

In Zen Buddhism we find many formulations expressing the inexpressibility of the highest principle, and the entire aim of the Zen effort is to shatter the attempt to understand the ultimate by means of discursive intelligence. (Cf. the writings of Daisetz T. Suzuki on Zen Buddhism, which are by far the best source for understanding its fundamental ideas. Precisely because of their authenticity Suzuki's books require more effort from the reader than a number of less authentic and "easier" books.)

In the Near East the concept of the One was expressed in the symbol of God *the supreme king*. This was a historical necessity, because in small states ruled by oriental despots who claimed for themselves divine power, the concept of the highest principle, of the One, had to be formulated in the symbol of the supreme king, the "King of Kings." To be sure, this God was different from all idols: He had no name and no image was permitted—or possible—to be made of him. As I pointed out in *You Shall Be as Gods* (1966), God made a concession to Moses, who said that unless he mentioned God's name the people would not believe him; and Moses mentioned his name. But the name itself was in an imperfect form (like a process and not a thing) and was best translated as "My name is nameless."

But in spite of these precautions, the symbol of God the king lent itself to the danger of anthropomorphization and an idolization of the concept of God. This danger was all the greater as the concept of God was cultivated by the Church in the European Middle ages, whose social structure was also dominated by the presence of emperors, popes, and feudal lords who were supreme figures. Thus the *symbol* "God"—standing for the One and the supreme value—deteriorated to an imagined *reality* of a King of Kings who ruled the rulers and their subjects from his supreme throne in heaven.

While this idolization of God dominated the concepts of the masses and those leaders who thought like the masses, there were always thinkers and groups (usually revolutionary ones) who wanted to cleanse the pure concept of the One from the "unclean," authoritarian, and idolized admixtures that had covered and distorted it. The history of Judaism and Christianity can be characterized as the continuing effort of restoring the concept of God to its original meaning.

"Negative theology" is an important manifestation of this effort; its most radical expression is found in mysticism and perhaps nowhere more boldly than in Meister Eckhart's thought.

Eckhart opposed all anthropomorphological admixtures of the god concept by opposing to it the concept of the Godhead, which is identical with the One = No-thing of Eastern thinking. In the frame of thought of his time a concept that there was no god, was unthinkable. By replacing God the Creator as supreme power with the Godhead, Eckhart could express the concept of the One in full purity.

If one considers this liberating function of Eckhart's mysticism and his uncompromising insistence on independence, one may be well prepared to correct the other cliché about mysticism: its being "irrational" and "opposed to reason."

"If God had no goodness, my will would not want him. . . . I am not blessed, because God is good; I also never want to desire that God gives me blessedness by his goodness, because he would not be able to. *I am blessed only because God is reason and because I recognize this.*" Or: "Reason is God's temple. Nowhere does God dwell more essentially than in his temple, in reason." (Both quotations are from the sermon *Quasi stella matutina,* cited by J. Quint; my translation; emphasis added.)

Many other statements by Eckhart could be added to these which show clearly that for Eckhart God *is* reason, not even love and goodness, and that man's supreme faculty is reason. That mysticism, with its radical renunciation of any thoughts or images *about* God, was not in conflict with rationality. No one recognized this with greater clarity than Albert Schweitzer, who expressed this idea in a statement that mysticism was the last consequence of rationalism.

As for the notion of Eckhart as an otherworldly man, withdrawn from society and practicing meditation all day, many statements in Eckhart's sermons clearly refute this image. One of the clearest expressions about man's activity is to be found in Eckhart's description of the "just one." Eckhart believed there were only a few just ones in the world but that they existed; Quint, summarizing Eckhart's statements, describes them as follows:

> They are difficult to recognize, these just and perfect ones of Meister Eckhart: If they feel the need, they eat, while other people [those who believe in the efficacy of good and saintly works] fast; they sleep when others stay awake; they are silent when others pray; briefly, all their words and works are uncomprehended by the crowd, for these just ones know that all those who do fast and stay awake much and do great [holy] works, without changing their mistakes and their conduct of life, betray themselves and are the devil's mockery. But there is one criterion by which the just ones can be recognized without fail by everybody: by their attitude toward their fellow men, toward the community. They never withdraw from their socioethical duty and action. Such a man is all men; he has broken through the barriers of the ego and of self-sufficiency; he does not know any more selfishness, the essential vice of this world. The honor of his fellow men, his joys, and his cares are his own.[1]

Quint ends his description of Eckhart's overall goals, summarizing them in this sentence: "To liberate the *essential* man, the just one, for *essential* work in a world freed to live in its *essential* being, so that this man becomes an active, useful servant of the community—this is Eckhart's effort throughout a long life of battle, a life of unerring passionate decisiveness, defying all obstacles."

If this description of Eckhart's goal were applied to Marx's views in the *Economic and Philosophical Manuscripts* of 1844, one would hardly do any injustice to Marx's ideas. Saying this does not, of course, mean to neglect the fact that Marx's were mainly concerned with the question *how* the world could be "freed

---

1. J. Quint, *Deutsche Predigten und Traktate,* trans. and ed. J. Quint, Munich, 1969, pp. 42ff.

to live in its essential being," while these questions about the economic and social conditions for essential being were not in Eckhart's field of vision. Nevertheless, Marx's views, while concentrating on economic analysis, do not contradict Eckhart's picture of the social, altruistic, active man, but presuppose it.

Atheistic Religiosity

Eckhart's mystical theology was one step in the historical process of liberating the idea of God from its anthropomorphic authoritarian admixture. With the growth of the natural sciences, of technique, and the beginning of the new individualism—and eventually the anti-authoritarian trend that culminated in the French Revolution—the traditional concept of God indeed became more and more vulnerable. One did not need God to explain the miracles of creation, and one needed God even less as the fountainhead of ethics. With the development of capitalism, economic relations between men, the most important sector of ethical behavior, became separated from man; economic behavior was not part of morals anymore, but was entirely determined by the laws of economy. Classic economy had become independent of man's will, intentions, and ethical norms. It had its own laws according to which the economic process proceeded, and man's behavior was determined by these laws.

"Deism" was a further step to get rid of the "King of Kings," without losing the word God entirely, but making the assumption that God had once started the world and after this event had stopped interfering and left it to its own devices. In the final analysis, this meant to the laws of economics.

The slow deterioration of religion had the effect that official religion, represented by the Church, represented the authoritarian ideas containing the "King of Kings" concept, and religion became a bulwark for political and economic reaction—essentially because the Church supported all reactionary elements in society. Hence, all words that were used by the Church became tabu for a revolutionary thinker such as Marx; and the concept of God, even if deprived of its authoritarian meaning, became an unspeakable word in any shape or form. But even words such as love, justice, and truth slowly acquired a tabu character because they were used by those Jung-Hegelians who claimed one could change the world by only changing man's consciousness. (Cf. Marx's and Engels' polemics in the "Introduction" to *The German Ideology*.[2]

Thus, Marx was under the same culturally conditioned pressures as Eckhart had been, only in reverse. For Eckhart a world picture without at least the word God was unthinkable; for Marx a world picture that contained words of religion and of philosophical idealism was equally unthinkable or, perhaps more correctly, to be avoided in theoretical discourse. If Marx had been allergic to religious words, however, would the student Marx have attended a course of lectures on the prophet Isaiah as the only non-obligatory course in his study plan? Would he, many years later, have told his wife, who was interested in attending some lectures by a very liberal minister: "If you really are interested in religion, read the prophets instead of listening to banalities." Indeed, Marx had great and empathic understanding for the essence of religion, an attitude that has been completely distorted by vulgar Marxism and has been borne out by his statement on religion, from which only one sentence, taken out of context, is widely quoted: "Religion is the opium of the people." I quote below the whole statement, which shows how different Marx's attitude to religion was from the one that is judged to be expressed in the "opium sentence":

> *Religious* distress is at the same time the *expression* of real distress and the *protest* against real distress. Religion is the sigh of the oppressed creature, the heart of a heartless world, just

---

2. K. Marx and F. Engels, MEGA, Vol. 5.

as it is the spirit of an unspiritual situation. It is the *opium* of the people.

The abolition of religion as the *illusory* happiness of the people is required for their *real* happiness. The demand to give up the illusions about its condition is *the demand to give up a condition which needs illusions.* The criticism of religion is, therefore, *in embryo the criticism of the vale of woe, the halo of which is religion.*

Criticism has plucked the imaginary flowers from the chain not so that man will wear the chain without any fantasy or consolation, but so that he will shake off the chain and cull the living flower. The criticism of religion disillusions man, to make him think and act and shape his reality like a man who has been disillusioned and has come to reason, so that he will revolve around himself and therefore around his true sun. Religion is only the illusory sun, which revolves around man as long as he does not revolve around himself. (Cf. K. Marx, *Toward the Critique of Hegel's Philosophy of Right.*)[3]

What Marx is saying here is that man suffers in a heartless world and that religion consoles him, as opium consoles one who suffers from severe pain. But religion is the necessary and best comfort for man's suffering only as long as man has not come to himself, as long as he lives in a world that requires illusions in order to be bearable. When Marx speaks of man's "culling the living flower," he conveys the idea that the aim of life is not the drabness of making a living but the beauty of being. To Marx, in a socialist society, when man has become fully himself, there is no need for religion, because the flowering quality of life will be expressed in the whole of daily life and not in a separate and necessarily alienated sector of life: religion.

When Marx speaks of the new man who becomes his own sun, he implies that, instead of God's being his sun, he fully negates the alienated idol "God," as already Eckhart had done, and he reestablishes the principles of humanism: "Man is the

---

3. Ibid., Vol 1, pp. 607ff.

measure of all things." But—and this is very important in order to avoid a widespread misunderstanding—for Marx this does not mean to make man into a god. This would only mean to transform man into the same alienated idol into which God has been transformed.

Indeed, the idolization of man is actually what has happened in the development of modern industrialism, and with increasing rapidity in the last decades. By knowing the secrets of nature, man feels that he becomes omniscient; and by controlling nature, he becomes omnipotent. The creation of nature by God is followed by the creation of a *second* nature by man. The denial of God is followed by the elevation of man into the role of God. This process was not conscious as such; it *could* not be conscious, because morality on which bourgeois society was built was still embedded in religious concepts. Indeed, as Dostoevski already recognized, if God were dead, everything would be allowed!

What would happen to civil society if everything was allowed? The traditional religious cover had to be preserved in order to guarantee the effectiveness of concepts such as duty, loyalty, patriotism, respect for law. Underneath this conscious cover, however, man was fired and sustained by the new vision of himself as God. Not he as an individual—who, in fact, sensed his powerlessness—but his society or, rather, the technically advanced sector of humanity, the white world of Europeans and North Americans. This new paganism, in which man became an idol, contained the deepest psychological motivation for the energy and skill that were necessary to construct the world of modern technique.

Indeed, the vision behind modern industrialism (capitalist as well as communist) was a religious one, as all visions are that mobilize the energies for new creative structures. Driven by this vision or, if you like, drunk with it, man performed the miracles of technique that he dreamt of, or even did not dream of, in his previous history. Has space travel not made him the creature of the universe, eliminating the limitations of space? Has he not acquired the possibility of changing the structure of the brain and altering reactions that seemed to be fixed by God's Creation? Are not the secret services, which can photograph and listen in to the most private happenings, as omniscient as one once believed God to be?

In fact, man is on the way to becoming God—or so he believes—and this is his answer to the religious tradition and the basis for a complete negation of ethics. Yet in order to become God, man has to become un-human—and thus in the long run to destroy himself by sacrificing himself at the altar of the true God to whom eventually the Man-God will have to abdicate: *technique.*

What Marx—like all radical humanists—meant by the ideas that "man should become his own sun" and that "man is the measure of all things" was not the idea of man as an idol; but that man, by being fully human, would fulfill the highest aim man should set for himself. We see here a new connection with Eckhart's mysticism. Eckhart said that man *is* God, or that God is in man—a statement that was one of the main reasons for the accusation of heresy against him. Eckhart did not refer to the god of the Bible, God the Creator, God the Authority. To him man was the Godhead, the One, the inexpressible; man's essence was pure being as the Godhead's essence was pure being. Hence, it could not be grasped, described, named; it was the One—and the No-thing. (This is what distinguishes Eckhart from many other mystics who speak of the *union* between man and God. Eckhart speaks of the union too, but he takes a decisive step beyond this concept: There is no need for union, since man and God are already one.)

There is little difference, except in terminology, between Eckhart's atheistic mysticism and Marx's concept of man as the highest being for himself. Both are atheistic, both speak against the idolization of man, for both the fulfillment of man lies in the unfolding of his essential power as a purpose in itself. If

Eckhart was an atheistic mystic speaking in the language of theology, Marx was an atheistic mystic speaking in the language of post-Hegelian philosophy. They spoke two different dialects of the same language, as far as man and the goal of man's life are concerned; as far as politics and economics are concerned, Eckhart did not speak in any language, while Marx's language was that of the classical economists.

General remarks on Marx's relationship to religion are almost unavoidably afterthoughts to the main topic: Marx's and Eckhart's views on *having* and *being*. What we have is much too sketchy and brief to deal with the problem Marxism and religion adequately. In a masterful way this has been done by Ernst Bloch, particularly in his *Atheismus im Christentum*. Bloch, with great sensitivity and often in a beautiful, poetic language, points to the atheistic character of true Christianity—the first Christians were called *atheoi* at Nero's court!—and formulates convincingly the apparent paradox: "Only an atheist can be a good Christian, but certainly also only a Christian can be a good atheist."[4] This paradox—a challenge in the book's Introduction—is developed and resolved in the later text. The conclusion at which Bloch arrives is, in general terms, the same as I have briefly formulated with respect to the thought of Eckhart and Marx: unalienated Christianity and unalienated Marxism proclaim the same principle. Bloch writes: "When, in Christian terms, one really still is concerned with the emancipation of the weary and downtrodden; when in Marxist terms the depth of the realm of freedom remains—and becomes—the true substance of revolutionary consciousness, then the alliance between revolution and Christianity of the peasant wars will not have been the last one—and this time it will succeed. . . . Then Marxism and the dream of the un-conditioned *(Unbedingten)* will unite in the same step and strategy."[5]

---

4. E. Bloch, *Atheismus im Christentum: Zur Religion des Exodus und des Reichs,* Frankfurt am Main, 1968, p. 24.

5. Ibid., pp. 353ff.

Bibliography

Aristotle. *Ethica Nicomachea*. London, New York, Toronto: Oxford University Press, 1942.

Baader, F. von. *Sämtliche Werke* [Complete Works], ed. F. Hoffman, 16 vols., 1851–60; reprinted by Nachdruck, 1963.

Becker, C. L. *The Heavenly City of the Eighteenth Century Philosophers*. New Haven, CT: Yale University Press, 1932.

Blakney, R. B. *Meister Eckhart: A Modern Translation*. New York: Harper and Row, 1941.

Bloch, E. *Atheismus im Christentum: Zur Religion des Exodus und des Reichs*. Frankfurt am Main: Suhrkamp Verlag, 1968.

Brzezinski, Z. "The Technotronic Society," in *Encounter*, Vol. 30 (January 1968), p. 19.

Butler, S. *The Way of All Flesh*. London, 1903. Also Butler, S. *Weg des Fleisches*, 2 vols. Vienna: Phaidon Verlag, 1929.

Cassirer, E. *Die Philosophie der Aufklärung*. Tübingen: Verlag Mohr, 1932.

Dionysius Areopagita (Pseudo). *Mystische Theologie und andere Schriften. Mit einer Probe aus der Theologie des Proklus*, ed. J. Gebser. Munich: Otto Wilhelm Barth-Verlag, 1956.

Eckhart, Meister. *Deutsche Predigten und Traktate*, ed. and trans. J. Quint. Munich: Carl Hanser Verlag, 1969.

Feuer, L. S. *Marx and Engels*. New York: Doubleday Anchor, 1959.

Fichte, J. G. *J. G. Fichtes Werke*, 6 vols., ed. F. Medicus. Leipzig: Felix Meiner, 1911.

Fromm, E. *Gesamtausgabe* [Collected Works], ed. R. Funk. Stuttgart: Deutsche Verlags-Anstalt, 1980–81; Munich: Deutscher Taschenbuch Verlag, 1989.

———. "Über Methode und Aufgabe einer Analytischen Sozialpsychologie: Bemerkungen über Psychoanalyse und historischen Materialismus," in

Zeitschrift für Sozialforschung (Leipzig: Hirschfeld Verlag), Vol. 1 (1932), pp. 28–54. Also in *Gesamtausgabe,* Vol. 1, pp. 37–57.

———. *Escape from Freedom.* New York: Farrar and Rinehart, 1941.

———. *Man for Himself: An Inquiry into the Psychology of Ethics.* New York: Rinehart and Co., 1947.

———. *The Sane Society.* New York: Rinehart and Winston, Inc., 1955.

———. *Sigmund Freud's Mission: An Analysis of His Personality and Influence,* Vol. 21 of *World Perspectives,* ed. Ruth Nanda Anshen. New York: Harper and Row, 1959.

———. *Marx's Concept of Man* (with a translation of Marx's *Economic and Philosophical Manuscripts* by T. B. Bottomore). New York: Continuum (A Frederick Ungar Book), 1961.

———. *Beyond the Chains of Illusion: My Encounter with Marx and Freud,* in *Credo Perspectives,* ed. Ruth Nanda Anshen. New York: Simon and Schuster, 1962.

———. "Humanism and Psychoanalysis," in *Contemporary Psychoanalysis,* Vol. 1 (1964), pp. 69–79.

———. *The Heart of Man: Its Genius for Good and Evil,* Vol. 12 of *Religious Perspectives,* ed. Ruth Nanda Anshen. New York: Harper and Row, 1964.

———. *You Shall Be as Gods: A Radical Interpretation of the Old Testament and Its Tradition.* New York: Holt, Rinehart and Winston, 1966.

———. "Die Grundpositionen der Psychoanalyse," in *Fortschritte der Psychoanalyse: Internationales Jahrbuch zur Weiterentwicklung der Psychoanalyse* (Göttingen: Verlag für Psychologie Hogrefe), Vol. 2 (1966), pp. 19–32. Also in *Gesamtausgabe,* Vol. 8, pp. 35–45.

———. Introduction to *The Nature of Man,* ed. E. Fromm and R. Xirau. New York: Macmillan, 1968. Also in *Gesamtausgabe,* Vol. 9, pp. 375–91.

———. "Marx's Contribution to the Knowledge of Man," in *Social Science Information* (The Hague, Netherlands), Vol. 7 (1968), pp. 7–17. Also in *Gesamtausgabe,* Vol. 5, pp. 421–32.

———. "Eine post-marxsche und post-freudsche Gedanken über Religion und Religiosität," in *Concilium: Internationale Zeitschrift* (Einsiedeln, Switzerland: Benziger/Grünewald), Vol. 8 (1972), pp. 472–76. Also in *Gesamtausgabe,* Vol. 6, pp. 293–99.

———. *The Anatomy of Human Destructiveness.* New York: Holt, Rinehart and Winston, 1973.

———. *To Have Or to Be?,* Vol. 50 of *World Perspectives,* ed. Ruth Nanda Anshen. New York: Harper and Row, 1976.

———. *The Art of Being.* New York: Continuum, 1992. Translated from *Vom Haben zum Sein: Wege und Irrwege der Selbsterfahrung,* ed.

R. Funk. Weinheim, Germany, and Basel, Switzerland: Beltz Verlag, 1989.

———. *Ethik und Politik: Antworten auf aktuelle politische Fragen,* ed. R. Funk. Weinheim, Germany, and Basel, Switzerland: Beltz Verlag, 1990.

———. *Die Pathologie der Normalität: Zur Wissenschaft vom Menschen,* ed. R. Funk. Weinheim, Germany, and Basel, Switzerland: Beltz Verlag, 1991; this volume includes Fromm's 1974 work "Is Man Lazy by Nature?" (translated into German as *Ist der Mensch von Natur aus faul?),* pp. 145–97.

Goethe, J. W. von. *West-österlicher Divan* [known as the Poetry Collection], ed. German Academy of Sciences of Berlin, Vol. 2. Berlin: Akademic Verlag, 1952.

Herder, J. G. *Ideen zur Philosophie der Geschichte der Menschheit,* in Herder's *Sämtliche Werke* [Complete Works], Vol. 13, ed. B. Suphan. Berlin, 1877ff.

Hesiod. *Sämtliche Gedichte* [Complete Poems], trans. W. Marg. Zurich and Stuttgart: Artemis Verlag, 1970.

Huxley, A. *Brave New World.* London: Vanguard Library, 1946.

Kahn, H. *On Thermonuclear War.* Princeton, NJ: Princeton University Press, 1960.

———. *The Year 2000: A Framework for Speculation on the Next Thirty-Three Years.* New York: Macmillan, 1967.

Korff, H. A. *Geist der Goethezeit,* 4 vols. Leipzig: Koehler und Amlang, 1958.

Lao-Tse. *Tao-Te-King: Das heilige Buch vom Weg und von der Tugend,* trans. G. Debon, Stuttgart: Philipp Reclam jun., 1967.

Lobkovicz, N. *Theory and Practice: History of a Concept from Aristotle to Marx.* Notre Dame, IN, and London: University of Notre Dame Press, 1967.

Marx, K. *Die deutsche Ideologie;* in *Historische-kritische Gesamtausgabe,* Vol. 5.

———. *Die Frühschriften,* ed. S. Landshut. Stuttgart: Kröner Verlag, 1971.

———. *Die heilige Familie;* in *Historisch-kritische Gesamtausgabe,* Vol. 3.

———. *Das Kapital;* in *Karl Marx und Friedrich Engels: Werek,* Vols. 23–25. Also *The Capital,* trans. E. Untermann. Chicago: Charles H. Kerr and Co., 1909.

———. *Zur Kritik der Hegelschen Rechtsphilosophie;* in *Historisch-kritische Gesamtausgabe,* Vol. 1.

———. *Manifest der kommunistischen Partei;* in *Historisch-kritische Gesamtausgabe,* Vol. 6. Also *The Communist Manifesto,* trans. S. T. Possony. Chicago: Henry Regnery Co., 1954.

———. *Ökonomisch-philosophische Manuskripten;* in *Historisch-kritische Gesamtausgabe,* Vol. 3.

————. and F. Engels. *Historisch-kritische Gesamtausgabe* [Collected Historico-Critical Works; MEGA], ed. V. Adoratsky. Part 1, 6 Vols. Berlin, 1932.

————. *Werke*, ed. Institute for Marxism-Leninism of the Central Committee of the German Socialist Unity Party. Berlin: Dietz Verlag, n.d.

Mauthner, F. *Der Atheismus und seine Geschichte in Abendlande*, Vol. 1. Stuttgart and Berlin: Deutsche Verlagsanstalt, 1920.

Mieth, D. *Die Einheit von vita activa und vita contemplativa in den deutschen Predigten und Traktaten Meister Eckharts und bei Johannes Tauler*, Vol. 15 of *Studien zur Geschichte der katholischen Moraltheologie*, ed. M. Müller. Regensburg: Verlag Friedrich Pustet, 1969.

————. *Christus, das Soziale im Menschen: Texterschliessungen zu Meister Eckhart*, Vol. 4. Düsseldorf: Patmos Verlag, 1972.

Mumford, L. *The Myth of the Machine: Techniques and Human Development.* New York: Harcourt Brace Jovanovich, 1967.

Nambara, M. *"Die Idee des absoluten Nichts in der deutschen Mystik une seine Entsprechungen im Buddhismus,"* in *Archiv für Begriffsgeschichte: Bausteine zu einem historischen Wörterbuch der Philosophie*, Vol. 6. Bonn: H. Bouvier, 1960, pp. 143–277.

Pfeiffer, F. *Meister Eckhart*, trans. and ed. F. Pfeiffer, Vol. 2 of *Deutsche Mystiker des 14. Jahrhunderts.* Fourth edition, Göttingen, 1924.

Quint, F. *Deutsche Predigten und Traktate,* trans. and ed. F. Quint. Munich: Carl Hanser Verlag, 1969.

Scholem, G. *"Zum Verständnis der Messianischen Idee im Judentum,"* in *Judaica.* Frankfurt am Main: Bibliothek Suhrkamp, Suhrkamp Verlag, 1963.

Schopenhauer, A. *Die Welt als Wille und Vorstellung*, Vol. 2 of *Werke*, ed. P. Deussen. Munich, 1911.

Sophocles. *Antigone*, in *Griechische Tragiker,* trans. K. W. F. Solger. Munich: Winkler-Verlag, n.d., pp. 313–54.

Spengler, O. *Untergang des Abendlandes,* 2 vols. Munich, 1918–22.

Stephenson, G. *"Gottheit und Gott in der spekulativen Mystik Meister Eckharts,"* dissertation, University of Bonn, 1954.

Stern, F. *Gold and Iron.* New York: Alfred A. Knopf, 1977.

Suzuki, D. T. *Mysticism: Christian and Buddhist*, Vol. 12 of *World Perspectives.* New York: Harper and Row, 1957.

Ueda, S. *Die Gottesgeburt in der Seele und der Durchbruch der Gottheit: Die mystische Anthropologie Meister Eckharts und ihre Konfrontation mit der Mystik des Zen-Buddhismus.* Gütersloh: Gütersloher Verlagshaus, G. Mohn, 1965.

Index

Printed in the United Kingdom by
Lightning Source UK Ltd., Milton Keynes
141468UK00001B/81/A